Sandy,

For your use of His Name.

Guy Berglund

USING JESUS'S NAME

USING JESUS'S NAME

GREG BERGLUND, M.D., M.DIV.

XULON PRESS ELITE

Xulon Press Elite
2301 Lucien Way #415
Maitland, FL 32751
407.339.4217
www.xulonpress.com

Printed in the United States of America.

ISBN-13: 978-1-54566-711-8

DEDICATION

To Patty, my beloved wife
and devoted mother of our children:
Kalley, Rose, Anne, and Tom.

ACKNOWLEDGEMENTS

Special thanks to my daughter, Annie, for her editing skills.

I am always so thankful for my lovely wife – her patience, wisdom, advice, prayers, and support.

Special thanks to those in our small fellowship group who share their gifts, encouragement, and prayers.

Thanks also to those participating in *Healing on the Hill*, a healing ministry at North Heights Lutheran Church.

All gratitude goes to God the Father, Jesus Christ His Son, and the Holy Spirit who work in us salvation, sanctification, empowering, and gifts for His glory and the work of the ministry.

TABLE OF CONTENTS

INTRODUCTION

The first time I heard and believed the great promise, "Ask anything in my Name and I will do it"[1], was when I went through a personal awakening and renewal of faith during my college years. My eyes were newly opened to the Word of God. The Holy Spirit was enlightening my understanding of these eternal Words of scripture.

After reading these words, I decided to ask of the Father in the Name of Jesus, just as the scriptural promise instructed. I asked for several rather simple and insignificant things which I do not remember now. Each of these requests were answered and provided by the Father, just as I had asked of Him in the Name of His Son Jesus.

This was great! What a great treasure I had learned from the Word of God.

Before long, actually it was a few days or weeks, those provisions did not keep coming as I had asked of the Father in the Name of Jesus. At least they did not come so quickly. My faith was not much shaken as I had just experienced a profound encounter with the Lord that overshadowed the simple little things I was asking of Him.

I continued to hours at a time studying and memorizing the Word of God. My prayers were answered at times but not consistently. I believed the Word of God but I was not experiencing everything it promised. My faith was solid, but my confidence in prayer was weakened as my experience at times was not consistent with what the Word of God promised.

REALIZED ESCHATOLOGY

For many believers this describes a typical progression and fluctuation of faith and confidence before God. For all of us there is both a "now" and a "not yet" experience of God's Word. Some promises and requests from God occur immediately or in timely fashion. Others are in waiting. They are not yet. Biblical theologians call this "realized eschatology," the simultaneous "now" and "not yet" tension of faith in which we all live.

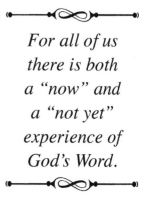

For all of us there is both a "now" and a "not yet" experience of God's Word.

This tension presents a choice to each of us, a decision that we regularly make, sometimes almost unconsciously: Will we ascribe to a theology that brings the Word of God down to our experience, or will we hold a theology that is based on the eternal truth of God's Word despite confirmation of our experiences? Will we evaluate and accept only those scripture verses that fit our experience, or will we trust and wait for the truths of scripture to become our experience? In simple words, will we believe our experience or God's Word?

By faith we lay hold of the promises of God. God has designed this process of faith to occur throughout a lifetime. To embrace the promise without the process misses the reality of appropriation and inheritance. The promise requires a process. Some promises of God are fulfilled

Will we believe our experience or God's Word?

in a span of time so that we learn to truly seek Him for who He is, not just what He does for us. We are to seek first the Kingdom of

God and His righteousness, and all these other needs will be added to us. How easily we actually seek first the added things instead.

As our hearts delight more in Him than what His promises bring to us, He in turn blesses us with the fulfillment of many great promises. His desire is for our hearts. "He yearns jealously over the spirit which he has made to dwell in us"[2].

The promise requires a process.

THE NAME GIVEN TO BELIEVERS

The Name of Jesus has great value and power. This Name is given to us to use in prayer and thanksgiving. We can confidently approach the Father's throne of grace when we do so in the Name of Jesus.

This great promise of the Word of God came from Jesus to His disciples and all who believe in Him: "Ask anything in my name, and I will do it"[3]. This appears to be a blank check that anyone can fill in.

But many do not receive what is asked of the Father, even when adding the supposed magical words "in Jesus's Name". After a few attempts with no provision, a certain crisis of faith may occur. Is the Word of God really true for me? Does this promise still function today?

The Apostle John spoke of a confidence we have when we ask anything in His Name. Most do not have this confidence in prayer. This is because we have not understood the Name of Jesus. We have not understood the scriptural importance of naming and especially the wonderful Name of Jesus.

We have ability to use the most powerful word of all times and places – the Name of Jesus – by which we can ask whatever desired and perform mighty deeds. Yet many misuse His great Name. Most Christians lack understanding and confidence of the power of this Name and how to effectively employ it according to instructions in the Word of God. What is it to abide in Him? How do Christians confidently use the Name of Jesus in prayer and ministry? What is it to believe on the Name, to believe in the Name, to believe the Name of Jesus?

A FOCUS ON THE NAME

Why does scripture so often refer to the Name rather than the person of the Lord? For example, in Ps. 124.8 we find these words: "Our help is in the name of the Lord, who made heaven and earth." This verse could say "Our help is in the Lord." This is a true statement – "He is our helper" - but the focus is on the Name of the Lord. The Name is where help is found. His Name is our help. This focus on the Name occurs repeatedly throughout the Word of God.

There are scriptures regarding praise and worship that speak of the Name of the Lord. Ps. 7.17 reads, "I will sing praise to the name of the Lord, the Most High," and Ps. 113.3 states, "From the rising of the sun to its setting the name of the Lord is to be praised." The Lord himself is worthy of praise and worship, which are directed to His Name.

Look at the benefits of knowing His Name as written in the Psalms: "Because he cleaves to me in love, I will deliver him; I will protect him, *because he knows my name*. When he calls to me, I will answer him; I will be with him in trouble, I will rescue him and honor him. With long life I will satisfy him, and show him my salvation" (Ps. 91.14-16, italics mine).

Why does scripture refer so frequently to the NAME of the Lord? We are to call upon the Name of the Lord. We can call upon the Lord, but we are to call upon His Name. We can worship and praise the Name of the Lord. Why is this expressed and accented in scripture? What is it about His Name?

This Name, the Name of the Lord, the Name Jesus, is given to us for our use, transmitting great power and carrying great meaning.

Using this Name wrongly brings guilt and judgment, while proper use brings great blessing and miraculous power. This Name has eternal significance.

What is it about the Name of the Lord, the Name of Jesus? How do we properly understand and use His Name?

CALLED BY HIS NAME

> If my people *who are called by my name* humble themselves, and pray and seek my face, and turn from their wicked ways, then I will hear from heaven, and will forgive their sin and heal their land (2 Chron. 7.14, italics mine).

Who are the people who are called by His Name? What does this mean? This scripture could state: *If my people who are called by me...* ; or, *If my people whom I call...* This familiar scripture states that the Name of the Lord calls His people.

The Word of God repeatedly focuses on the Name. Why is this so? This scripture does not just refer to God's people generically, but rather as an invitation to the people of God who are called by His Name. The Word of God here carefully describes God's people as those who are called by His Name, the ones whom He has called, whom He has foreknown, whom He has chosen, whom He has elected, justified, sanctified, and empowered. God's Name calls His people.

The Word of God repeatedly focuses on the Name.

When Paul was converted on the road to Damascus, he was called by the Name of Jesus. He did not see Jesus, but he was called by His Name. When Paul saw the great light and fell to the ground, he heard a voice saying, "Saul, Saul, why do you persecute me?" Paul responded, "Who are you,

Lord?" The reply: "I am Jesus, whom you are persecuting." Paul was thus called by the Name of the Lord Jesus. He did not see or feel Jesus, but he heard His Name. Paul's call was clarified and established by knowing the Name of the One who called him. Without Jesus's Name in this encounter, Paul would not know his calling or Who it was that called him. Thus God's people are called by His Name.

We can understand the biblical function of a name. We can know the One whose Name is above every other name. We can use the Name of Jesus as His Name is upon us and given to us. We can have confidence in prayer by properly understanding and employing the Name of Jesus. We can do everything in the Name of Jesus. We can thank the Father for everything in the Name of Jesus. We can ask the Father in the Name of Jesus.

My objective for writing this book is simply to know, understand, and properly use the Name of Jesus. Here I set out to find an answer for why the scriptures focus not just on the Lord Himself, but on His Name. Why do we praise the *Name* of Jesus? Why does the Psalmist say, "Blessed be the *Name* of the Lord"?[4] What instructions, benefits, callings, and authorities are linked to this Name? How do we properly use the Name of Jesus?

This book is arranged in four parts in an effort to restore the confidence we have in Him by understanding, knowing, and properly using the great, beautiful, wonderful, and powerful Name of Jesus: 1) What is a name?; 2) Names for God; 3) Jesus's Name; and 4) Use the Name. The first section establishes the meanings and functions of a name. The next two sections focus on the Names of the Triune God and an understanding of meaning and power in the Name of Jesus. The last section is devoted to proper, faith-filled, scriptural usage of the great Name of Jesus.

My hope for all who read this is that you will be brought to increased insight into the Word of God by the inspiration of the Holy Spirit. Heaven and earth will pass away, but the Word of God abides forever. This book is written to bring you to encounter with the eternal book, the Word of God. May God bless you and increase your faith and confidence in Him in reading this book.

SECTION ONE

———◦(∞)◦———

WHAT IS A NAME?

The first section of this book sets forth a foundation of understanding the functions and roles of names in our regular usage of them. The Bible uses names extensively for descriptive and prescriptive purposes. The Word of God repeatedly assigns strategy, benefits, and power to the Names of God. An understanding of the biblical usages of names gives us strategies for properly using the Name of Jesus.

Chapter 1

THE NEED FOR A NAME

A NAME GIVEN

"Do you like your name?" My mother asked me when I was six or seven years old. Until then I had never thought about it. Not knowing quite how to answer her at the time, I timidly responded, "Yes, I like my name." Her question awakened my curiosity. Why was I named Greg? My middle name is Gerald, and while it is my father's given name, I had not yet reflected why it was given to me. My young mind had hardly engaged with semantics, but I considered that, possibly, Greg and Gerald sounded alike and, therefore, were chosen by my parents. Later I learned that the name Greg means "watchful" or "vigilant" (γρηγορεω, Greek). My parents were not aware of the etymology of this name when it was given to me. Nevertheless, my name inspires me to fulfill its meaning.

As for most people, my name was there before I could remember. I have never thought about whether I liked it or not, nor of changing my name. If I were required to change my name, I would have no idea what name to choose because my name is firmly set in my identity. Others know me by my name. My given name calls forth an identity with memories in those who know me. Those who change their given name will remove, to certain extent, the connections that memories and associations afforded in the past.

3

My wife and I are blessed to birth and raise four children. As usual in our culture, we named each one with a first name and a middle name. This was not an easy decision. Much discussion about names occurred during the pregnancy of each child. What female or male name would carry well throughout the course of a long life? What name is distinct enough, yet not easily misunderstood or ridiculed? What name will fit well in infancy, childhood, young adulthood, adulthood, and to the end of life? What are the meanings of the names considered and what blessings or identity might this confer upon the child?

We have also named several pets, an easier task in theory, but sometimes just as taxing with four children's opinions. Pets usually do not take a job unless functioning as a service pet or in law enforcement - so its name is given for purposes of establishing communication, interaction, and obedience to commands.

Had we not given a name to our children, we would have been relegated to using pronouns and adjectives, or pointing at the child if nearby. This would obviously not work well, with constant confusion as to who is being referenced. A labored effort would be required to ensure that we would be talking to or about the right child.

So we are created with a need for names. Names establish and communicate identity. They enable efficient conversation. Names serve to preserve memories of individuals.

Names establish and communicate identity.

In everyday life as we experience different places, concepts and people, the use of names is necessary for communication and meaning, as that is what our language was built to express.

A DIAGNOSTIC NAME

My primary employment is as a physician in an emergency department. One particular shift I saw a woman with low back pain, a situation particularly common among ER patients. This woman did not have an injury event to bring on her discomfort. She stated the pain radiated into her right buttock and part way down the back side of her upper leg. After finishing the visit and establishing a treatment plan, the nurse brought in discharge instructions for follow-up and a prescription for a non-narcotic pain reliever and a muscle relaxant.

At the time of her discharge she reported to the nurse some dissatisfaction with her visit. I had explained to her the nature of her back pain in simple terms. She came away thinking the diagnosis was back pain, which was an accurate diagnosis, but this was something she already knew before coming to see a doctor. To her the diagnosis of back pain did not legitimatize her symptoms and the outcome of my time with her.

The nurse then showed her the name of the diagnosis that was entered into her record and was written on her discharge papers. She was diagnosed with "lumbar radiculopathy." She did not know what this was exactly, but she was immediately satisfied. Now expressed in medical terminology, her pain and her visit were legitimized. Though her symptoms had not changed, she was now ready to go forth with the treatment plan because she had an official name for her condition.

Any of us may have some frustration if there is no name to describe what is causing certain symptoms. We want the name of a definitive diagnosis, even if this name does not direct a specific treatment plan. The assignment of a diagnostic name may at least bring some understanding and facilitate a connection with others.

We can be frustrated when no name describes anything or matter which pertains to us. A specific name allows communication to go beyond the generalities of referring to something as "that thing" or "what-cha-ma-call-it."

THE FIRST NAME SPOKEN

When did names first occur? Was it Adam who is the first person listed in the creation story? His name means "man," but Adam was also a name. His was the first human name in the biblical record. Was this the first name?

When was the first name spoken? It was BEFORE creation. The first name spoken occurred before creation. God spoke creation into existence. He did not just have a thought when He created matter. Creation occurred at the speaking of God's voice. The items that came into being did so because God called out a name. Though all things are possible with God, He chose to create all things by His word. His strategy for creation was to speak words. Creation began with God's spoken word which requires naming. Anyone who speaks must use nouns, all of which are names of people, places, or things. Language consists of nouns, verbs, and modifiers. All nouns are names. These are words we use to call something to mind.

The first name spoken occurred before creation.

On the first day of creation, God said, "Let there be light"; and there was light."[1] He separated the light from the darkness and called the light Day, and the darkness he called Night.[2]

Then the next day, day two of creation, God said, "Let there be a firmament in the midst of the waters, and let it separate the waters from the waters."[3] And God called the firmament Heaven.[4]

Then God gathered together the waters into one place and spoke words for dry land to appear. "God called the dry land Earth, and the waters that were gathered together he called Seas."[5]

So God had a name for light, heaven, earth, and seas. He spoke these names to bring them into being. In similar fashion and strategy God created all things by speaking words, including names. Creation happened as God spoke forth names and commands. So names existed before creation and began with God.

Then God created humans in His own image with an ability to speak, distinguishing them from animals with this unique feature. Many other living beings regularly communicate one with another, but they do not use words and the constructs of language. Adam and Eve and all humans, created in God's image, have the same ability to speak.

So naming began with God. He created humans in His image with the same ability to name things. "Then God brought every beast of the field and bird of the air to Adam to see what he would name them."[6] To this day we all, created in the image of God, have the same ability to name and to call things by name.

We benefit by understanding the place and power of a name. Why? Because we have capacity to use names; because God made the Name of His Son Jesus to be above every other name; because we can call on the Name of Jesus; because His Name is the key that unlocks present benefits and an eternal inheritance. The Name of Jesus is what makes all the promises of God come to you.

Chapter 2

AUTHORITY TO NAME

Language consists of nouns and verbs with modifiers. Nouns are people, places and things. Each of these has a name in each language. These names are given by humans. The names call forth a mental image or thought that enables speech and interactive communication.

Naming comes out of ability to communicate and speak. The ability to speak requires the use of names. Humans are unique, set apart from all other beings of creation, because of an ability to communicate with languages. This is how we are created in God's image: we have ability to speak. In the beginning, God spoke to create what exists out of nothing. As all spoken words are invisible sound waves, so God's invisible spoken words created all things. Everything visible began with

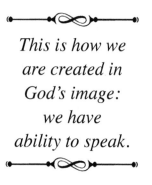

This is how we are created in God's image: we have ability to speak.

a word that included names. God said, "Let there be light," and there was light. An ability to speak with language and a name for light was employed by God to create.

The authority to *give* a name usually represents some authority *over* the thing or being that is receiving the name. This is true from the beginning, as God created the living creatures of the earth and brought them to Adam to see what he would name them. God gave humans authority over the earth and the creatures that dwell therein. So God did not name these, but brought them to Adam to see what he would name them. This was because He had delegated authority to Adam (humans) over these beings and things. This authority to name things is required for communication, is unique to humans, and functions as part of our being created in the image of God. This delegated authority given by God to people continues to this day.

Identifying something by name engages some degree of focus and power. Giving of a name is often done by someone holding some realm of authority. Parents name their children. Families name their pets. New discoveries are named by the discoverer or some overseeing entity. New inventions are named by their inventor. New businesses are named by their founders.

God created every beast of the field and every bird of the air, bringing them to man to see what he would call them. God gave humans dominion over the earth and all that dwells in it. The power and authority to name things is the first expression of this dominion God had given. God used words to name things; humans do the same as ones created in His image and given dominion over certain parts of God's creation.

Stating a name does not automatically place you in authority or control. However, if you are in a position of authority, calling the name of the person or thing does carry extra strength. Just as Jesus called His disciples by name and sought the name of the legion of demons, so believers have certain authority delegated by God whereby we can call certain things or beings by name (see Luke 17.5-6; Matt. 17.20).

THE MEANING OF A NAME

Think about your own name. What is your given name? What is its meaning? Was your name chosen because of its meaning

9

or for some other reason? What meaning does your name have to you? What power does it have over you? Do you have a nickname when you are at home, but not in the world at large? Or vice versa? How many names do you legally have? Why? Where did they come from? What do you think your name means to others when they hear it?

Have you ever been in position to give a name to another? Perhaps when you were young you named your stuffed animal. You could choose any name as you were one of just a few who would know and use that name. Maybe you named a pet dog or cat. These names will last for the duration of the life of the pet (and beyond as you recall memories), but the pet will not make any connection to the background meaning of the name or any associations the name may have in society. The dog or cat does not care what name you give, but does pick up on your attitudes and demeanor as you speak its name.

Giving a name to another person is a far more important task. The given name will stay with the person for their whole life, for decades. Will the name fit the person through all stages of life? Is it a name that can easily be ridiculed? Is the name previously used among certain relatives? Will the meaning of the name call forth certain traits? The answers to some of these questions may never be predicted.

These questions plagued my wife and me as we discussed naming our children, often going back and forth between options that one of us liked and one of us did not. Several names caught both of our attention, but we wanted to set eyes on each of our children before assigning their name for life.

A name is given to establish a reference to an identity. A person grows into the given name and the given name has meaning for identity and function. A person's words and actions contribute to a

A name is given to establish a reference to an identity.

10

good name or a bad name. A name carries with some direction for identity and function.

WILL YOU STAY IN YOUR POSITION?

Being raised in a small town, I was afforded opportunities to participate in all the sports, music, and drama offered in our school. For instance, I played football every fall season. As a junior and senior I started on the varsity team as a guard in the offensive line and on defense a middle linebacker. At the end of a Friday night varsity game the assistant coach, who coached the B squad, asked me if I could play in the B squad game the next morning. "Sure," I answered, but I wondered why he was pulling a varsity player into a B squad game. The opponent was from a town with a much larger school so I thought this might be his motivation.

The next morning I came to the locker room to get ready for the game. Another varsity player – a running back – was suiting up. As I went to talk with him, my younger brother, the B squad quarterback, joined in the conversation, expressing our curiosity at why we were playing in the B squad game.

Suddenly, a thought popped up that I jumped on with enthusiasm: "I would like to be a running back for a couple plays." This seemed good, albeit a bit devious, to the other two. I think it fueled some motivation, as we were sore from the previous night's game. We came up with a secret plan, keeping it on the hush even around the coaches. At some point in the second quarter, I would switch places with the running back and run a couple plays.

As the game unfolded, we followed our plan smoothly, my brother announcing the play in the huddle. The running back took his stance in the left guard position, and I took the backfield as a running back, my jersey displaying in bold number "75". The ball snapped to my brother who handed the ball to me for a gain of about seven yards. We went back to the huddle and the same play was called again. This time I scampered for another seven yards and a first down.

As I went back to the huddle, I heard another player calling my name as my substitute. I ran to the coach at the sideline who then told me to stand next to him. He did not say anything for the next three plays, as I stood anxiously considering the consequences. Was I in trouble? What was going to happen now? Maybe he liked my ability to run the ball. It also occurred to me that he might be thinking about his choices to bring varsity players into the B squad game.

He did not say anything to me while I stood by him for those three plays. Then he warned, "OK Berglund, if I put you back in the game, will you stay in your position?"

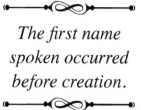

The first name spoken occurred before creation.

"Yes."

"OK," he said, "get in there." I returned to the huddle and thereafter stayed within my identity and position on that team.

Just as my number 75 indicated I was a lineman, so a person's name carries a certain identity and position for interactions in life.

Chapter 3

A NAME'S FUNCTIONS

DESCRIPTIVE AND PRESCRIPTIVE NAMES

Many names for people and places in the Bible, especially the Old Testament writings, are chosen because of their meanings or associations. The names themselves were otherwise regularly used to describe characteristics, circumstances, memories, attitudes, or events. The name itself calls this to mind and preserves certain memories. These are descriptive names, retroactively named AFTER some event, circumstances, memories, attributes, attitudes, or people. A child named after a relative is a descriptive name that refers back to another person and carries forward a link to certain memories and a certain heritage.

Prescriptive names serve to prescribe or call forth a certain identity with specific functions and attributes. These names have meaning for the future as there is a message in the name about a certain identity or function. So the giving of such names may be prophetic. When I learned my name means watchful and vigilant, this motivated me to embody those characteristics. My name was a sort of prescription for me to be observant. The meaning of any name can prescribe a specific identity or function.

DESCRIPTIVE NAMES OF PLACES

Descriptive names for places occurred frequently in the biblical record. After Moses led the people across the miraculously parted Red Sea, they went into the wilderness of Shur where for three days they were without water. They then arrived at a place that had water, but it was bitter. So the place was named "Marah" which in Hebrew means "bitter."[1]

The place where Abraham and Abimelech swore an oath was named Beersheba which means "the well of the oath."[2]

As the people wandered through the wilderness, they complained in the hearing of the Lord about their misfortunes and the anger of the Lord burned hotly, and the fire of the Lord burned among them until Moses prayed for the fire to abate. "So the name of that place was called Taberah, because the fire of the Lord burned among them."[3] "Taberah" is the Hebrew word for "burning."

DESCRIPTIVE NAMES OF PEOPLE

Similarly, names of people have meanings. Moses was so named by Pharoah's daughter because she drew him out of the water. Moses means "to produce" or "to draw forth." Moses was taken out of the water where he was placed in a basket by his mother who could no longer hide him from the Egyptian's King's edict to kill the Hebrews born male.

Jacob was so named because he was born holding the heel of his twin brother. Jacob means "heel grabber," "trickster," or "supplanter." Jacob's life followed the meaning of his name, perhaps unwittingly, as he tricked his brother out of his birthright. Later he wrestled with God about this heritage and identity until God changed his name. We will pick this up later in this chapter.

The vast majority of names for people listed in scripture, and of those for generations down through the ages, are chosen and decided by the parents. God instructed parents as to what name to give to their child in a few occasions in scripture (e.g. Isaac,

Ishmael, John the Baptist, Jesus, Hosea's children), yet it was still the parents who so named their child in obedience to God's instructions. So, even in these special circumstances, God did not bypass the authority he delegated to parents for naming their children.

PRESCRIPTIVE NAMES OF PEOPLE

Hosea

Hosea gave peculiar names to his children, which carried a prophetic message to the people of Israel. Hosea was a prominent, well-known, prophet in the land. God told Hosea to take a harlot in marriage and have children of harlotry. This was a prophetic action, a message to the people of Israel as they were committing great harlotry by forsaking the Lord. The message through Hosea's marriage to the harlot, Gomer, was one of grace and mercy. Though the people forsook the Lord, he yet embraced them intimately.

God then instructed Hosea to name his first child "Jezreel." This name means "God will scatter." Jezreel was the name of a fertile valley where Ahab and Jezebel brought about the murder of Naboth and where Jehu extinguished Ahab's house. Jehu accomplished God's purposes in taking down Ahab and Jezebel, but he himself had selfish motives and did not turn from idolatry to walk in the Law of Jehovah.[4]

This was the context in which Hosea had named his child Jezreel. So every occasion when Hosea may be talking with someone casually in the marketplace, where someone would ask his son's name, Hosea took the opportunity to prophecy to the people of Israel. He likely said something like this: This is my son, Jezreel, God will scatter, because God will scatter the house of Israel in the valley of Jezreel.

> And the Lord said to him, "Call his name Jezreel;
> for yet a little while, and I will punish the house of
> Jehu for the blood of Jezreel, and I will put an end

to the kingdom of the house of Israel. And on that day, I will break the bow of Israel in the valley of Jezreel" (Hos. 1.4-5).

Then Hosea and his wife Gomer had a second child, a girl, who God instructed to be named "Not Pitied," for God would no longer have pity on the house of Israel. Then a third child was born, a boy who was to be named "Not My People," for God was saying Israel was not His people and He was not their God. The names of Hosea's children bore a prophetic voice to the people of Israel calling each one to repent of their sins and return to the Lord.

So when Hosea took his children to get food and drink or when strolling about the area, each time he called their names there was a message delivered to others who heard him.

Their names made them preachers with a message.

What it would be like to grow up with these names "God Will Scatter," "Not Pitied," and "Not My People"? Imagine a roll call at school or some other event with names such as John, Kathy, James, Nicholas, Susan, Amy, Not Pitied, Frank, George, Lisa, Rebecca, and Not My People. These names would stand out each time they were uttered. They were a reminder to the people of their idolatry and God's discipline. These names were a life-long admonition of God's intervening judgments because Israel refused to hear and heed God's words.

Nothing is said of how Hosea's children fared. What would it be like for you to have one of these names? Certainly the Lord, who named them for purposes of prophesying to Israel, watched over them and attended to their souls.

John the Baptist

Zechariah and Elizabeth were instructed by God to name their son John. During Elizabeth's pregnancy Zechariah was unable to speak due to his disbelief of God's message through the angel. When their son was born, Elizabeth spoke forth his name as John. Others questioned her as this name bore no ties to family lineage. There were no descriptive reasons to name him John. Zachariah was consulted about this and wrote on a tablet that his name was to be John. Immediately his voice returned to him with ability to speak normally.[5] His written name enabled his spoken name.

This name "John" signifies "the grace of Jehovah." The giving of the name John to his son brought Zechariah's voice to return to him. He believed and was obedient to the Word of the Lord. At this time the Holy Spirit came upon Zachariah so he prophesied about John. When Zachariah believed and obeyed the Lord in naming his son John, the Holy Spirit empowered him to speak and prophesy. So John's name was not borne out of his family lineage, but given to him in obedience to God. His name was prescriptive and included prophetic words from Zechariah.

JESUS

Turning to the title and basis of this entire book, Jesus's Name was prescriptive, prophetic, and first given to his mother Mary. She was instructed by the angel what her Son's Name was to be. Here again, the Name Jesus was prescriptive and prophetic. That is to say, His very Name described who He was and would be. "And behold, you will conceive in your womb and bear a son, and you shall call his name Jesus. He will be great, and will be called the Son of the Most High; and the Lord God will give to him the throne of his father David, and he will reign over the house of Jacob forever; and of his kingdom there will be no end."[6] "You shall call his name Jesus, for he will save his people from their sins."[7] Mary was told by

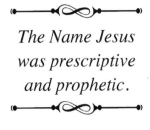

The Name Jesus was prescriptive and prophetic.

Gabriel what she was to call her son: "You are to call him Jesus."

The Name Jesus was prescriptive and prophetic, meaning "rescuer," "deliverer," "savior," "messiah," "one who saves." At the time of Jesus's birth, His Name described prophetically who He would be and what He would do. To this day and forever, His Name describes who He is, His position, what He has done, what He does, and what He will do. It was Mary and Joseph who so named Jesus in obedience to the word of God coming from Gabriel the angel.

A CHANGED NAME

Scripture records a few occasions in scripture where God changed a person's name. This was done to establish a new or enhanced identity and/or communicate a message through the meaning of the name. These new names carried a prophetic message woven into the name itself.

ABRAHAM AND SARAH

God changed the name "Abram" to "Abraham" and the name "Sarai" to "Sarah." In each name the change involved adding the Hebrew letter "hei (ה)," which is the fifth letter of the Hebrew alphabet. According to some Jewish scholars, the letter "hei" is connected to the divine breath or Spirit of God that releases His creative power and potential.

The message and meaning of this letter "hei," also representing the number five, is evident in the Hebrew text of Gen. 2.4 which says, "These are the generations of the heavens and the earth when they were created." The Hebrew word translated "created" is "bara," which means "created out of nothing." In this verse, "bara" has the letter "hei" inserted into it (barah) which is not a typical spelling and grammatical usage. No good grammatical reason exists for this word to include the letter "hei" except to communicate a deeper truth. Remember, the letter "hei" is often seen as the letter of the divine breath of God, which, along with the Word of God, is the means by which creation came to be: "By the word of the LORD the heavens were made, and all their host by the breath of his mouth" (Ps. 33.6). So the letter *"hei"* in the word translated "created" in Gen. 2.4 speaks of the divine breath or Spirit releasing God's creative power.

(This can give insight as to why David picked up five (*"hei"* is "five" in Hebrew) stones to go against Goliath. David relied upon the supernatural power of God's divine breath to overcome the enemy Goliath, to bring victory in war, and to restore honor to the Name of the Lord. David needed the *"hei,"* the divine empowerment of God's Spirit, to obtain victory and overcome what seemed impossible.)

This truth can also be seen in the life of Abram and Sarai. God promised they would conceive a child, but years went by without a fulfillment of this promise. As a sign they would bear children even in their old age, to fulfil God's promise to them, the Lord changed their names:

> Behold, my covenant is with you, and you shall be the father of a multitude of nations. No longer shall your name be Abram, but your name shall be Abraham; for I have made you the father of a multitude of nations (Gen. 17.4-5).

> And God said to Abraham, "As for Sarai your wife, you shall not call her name Sarai, but Sarah shall be her name. I will bless her, and moreover I will give you a son by her; I will bless her, and she shall be a mother of nations; kings of peoples shall come from her (Gen. 17.15-16).

The Lord changed Abram's name to "AbraHam," and Sarai's to "SaraH." These names have one Hebrew letter difference between their new names and their old ones – the addition of the letter *"hei,"*

19

or H in English. The Lord added this letter to their names because it represented His creative power to accomplish the impossible! Their new names provided prophetic direction and power for who they were and God's calling on their lives.[8]

JACOB

God also changed the name Jacob to Israel. Jacob means "trickster," "supplanter," or "heel grabber," since when he was born he was holding onto Esau's heel. It also means "may God be your rear guard." Esau, his older brother, carried the birthright, but sold it to Jacob when he was hungry for food. Though the birthright was therefore Jacob's, he seized it from Isaac unlawfully by pretending to be Esau. Jacob was in fact a crafty usurper, a trickster, as his name purports.

The Lord did not let Jacob's past define him, though Jacob struggled with God over his past and his identity. God forgave him and renamed him "Israel," meaning "God fights," "prince with God," or "power with God." Jacob was so named because he prevailed in his struggle with God. This struggle surrounded his disappointments and the consequences of past sins. He spent time with God over these matters to break through and go beyond them. Jacob admitted his guilt and absolute dependence on God, clinging to Him with all his might for the blessing he knew God would bring.

These different names were given to people as a blessing from the Lord, to signify something about them, their nature or their life, had changed in some way. Jesus Himself gave a new name to one of the twelve disciples when He called them and named them as apostles. Simon was given the name Peter (petra, which means rock). Later Jesus called Saul whose name was changed to Paul. This is discussed further in the next chapter.

A FAMILY NAME

The biblical names we just discussed are given names. There were no surnames or last names in the biblical record. Rather they were known as the sons or daughters of their father. Lot was the son of Haran, Abraham's brother. Rachel was the daughter of Laban.

Generally in most cultures today, having a last name or surname is typical. These names also communicate additional identity and heritage. Those ancestors before us have blazed a path able to generate a family identity. Siblings and cousins with the same family name indicate connections as blood relatives. A family name may give clues regarding geographical and nationality origins.

At marriage most brides take on the family name of the one they marry. Marriage involves leaving the father and mother and cleaving to their husband.[9] Asking a married woman her maiden name uncovers insight into her heritage and identity from her family of origin.

The Word of God states every family name is given by God the Father. "For this reason I bow my knees before the Father, from whom every family in heaven and on earth is named."[10] Your family name ultimately comes from God.

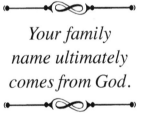

Your family name ultimately comes from God.

When my paternal great grandparents came from Sweden, they took the opportunity to change their last name to Berglund. Their last name in their home town in Sweden was the same as a notorious horse thief. Understandably, they no longer wanted that association despite moving an ocean away from that home town.

There are many similar stories where a family name is changed. Some cultures do not use a surname, only a first name for identification. Others may have numerous names, four or five or more. In all these families, in fact all families on earth and in heaven, their names are nevertheless ultimately derived by God as stated in Eph. 3.14-15.

A name depicts certain characteristics, qualities, and attributes. Mention of a name evokes memories, perspectives, and emotions. The Greek word for name is "*onoma*" (ονομα); the Hebrew word is "*shem*" (שֵׁם). The Greek "onoma" means name, character, reputation, the manifestation or revelation of someone's character so as to distinguish them from all others. According to Hebrew perspectives, a name is inseparable from the person to whom it belongs, something of the essence of that person.

The value of a name is to be preserved and maintained among others. A person's name is to be guarded for who the person really is. Names were so important to God that He devoted two of the Ten Commandments to preserving the honor and dignity of a name: the third commandment preserves God's holy Name (do not take the Lord's Name in vain[11]); the ninth preserves others names (do not bear false witness[12]).

A person's name is to be guarded for who the person really is.

Chapter 4

THE POWER OF NAMES

CALLING A NAME

When you call out someone's name you are engaging a beckon that captures that person's attention. If a person overhears his name spoken, you are making that person turn towards you every time that name is mentioned. If a person is not listening, even if involved in another conversation, the moment you say that person's name he or she will drop or suspend the current conversation and direct attention toward you. Teachers may use this to great effect in a classroom, but this happens for whoever may call another person's name regardless of position of authority.

Depending on the context of the conversation, if you say a person's name followed with talk filled with pride, happiness, disappointment, praise, or shame, it will be heard. When attention is turned to you this person will immediately pick up on the feelings with which you have associated his or her name. The use of a name will ensure a remembrance of what feelings were evoked. Is this not power, the ability to directly purvey your feelings to someone by use of a name? We see this power of calling by name in regular human interactions. This is a very common occurrence happening many times daily for virtually every person.

NICKNAMES

Some people acquire a nickname which may be a shorter version of their first or last name. A nickname also may be derived from any other characteristic, personality trait, or event. It seems nicknames are more frequent during adolescence and school years and may function alongside the identity formation occurring during development. For whatever reason nicknames occur, they also have some power in describing or shaping one's identity.

Is this not power, the ability to directly purvey your feelings to someone by use of a name?

JOE AVERAGE

When high school classes resumed in September in my small hometown, we could all immediately notice the student who was new in the community. In classic teenage fashion, many students speculated about the student's background and abilities. Was he an athlete that could help our team or was he one who might take my place and put me on the bench? Was he a good student? Which social group or clique will he likely fit into?

The answers circulating to these questions about him often included the word "average." He was an average student. He was average in sports. He had average height and weight. The report about this new student was that he was average. We learned that his first name was "Joe." So he quickly became known as "Joe Average." He seemed to embrace this nickname and ordered an athletic jersey with "Joe Average" written on the upper back. After a month or two he had a girlfriend. For the record she was average too.

CRUD

When one leaves home to attend college or university, it becomes a new beginning of sorts with the introduction of more independence and responsibilities. All freshman students are in this same transition. The switch from high school to college is a distinct reset at which time you may acquire a new nickname, lose your nickname, or continue on with the current name.

There was one classmate of mine who introduced himself as "Crud." I chuckled as I heard this peculiar nickname coming directly from him. I asked for his given name. He said it was Jim, but I should call him Crud. After a rather short time Crud became well-known on campus because of his nickname. Everyone greeted him as Crud and referred to him as Crud. It seemed not many people knew his real name.

Crud also acted out his nickname identity to some degree. He dressed like crud. He looked a little like crud. It seemed he did not bathe often. His hair was shaggy and his face had a scraggly beard. His attitudes and comments were also fitting with his nickname at times. This was Crud. His name defined who he was and everyone who called him by the name Crud reinforced this role he apparently chose for himself.

It is not that Christ came into existence before Abraham did, but that He never came into being at all.

He continued in this role with this nickname for his freshman, sophomore, and junior years of college. We all returned after a summer break to resume classes for our senior year. I noticed someone at a distance, perhaps twenty-to-thirty yards away. He looked familiar, and I thought I recognized him but was not sure. On a few other occasions during our first days back to school, I saw this somewhat familiar-looking man but I did not dare ask him for his name because I thought he might be Crud. He did not look like Crud and I did not want to mistakenly call him a demeaning nickname. I asked someone I thought might know, "Is that Crud?"

"Yes, he replied, "that's Jim."

Like most everyone else, I had forgotten his true name.

I learned he had become a Christian that summer. His life was changed by the transforming grace of God. He cleaned up, dressed nicely, and lost some weight. He no longer looked or acted like crud AND no one called him Crud any longer. He was known as Jim to everyone. He lost his nickname.

What was it like for him to hear his nickname throughout these years? This well-known nickname came at a price to his self-image. He was trapped somewhat in the image he had lived as Crud. It seems he had to get away from us for that summer in order for the Lord to make a change in his life.

That senior year everyone called him "Jim." No one called him Crud any longer because that nickname no longer fit him. He had to undergo a transformation in order for us to lose his nickname. That first day I met him when he requested I call him Crud, I could have chosen to refer to him as Jim rather than reinforce something unedifying. What would have happened with Jim if we had all recognized the power of a name and refused to call him something he was not? We could have spoken truth to him to affirm and establish a better identity.

> Let no evil talk (unwholesome words) come out of your mouths, but only such as is good for edifying, as fits the occasion, that it may impart grace to those who hear (Eph. 4.29, parentheses mine).

Calling out a name carries great power. Any associations or attitudes that are attached to the speaking of a name are also communicated. These can be powerful to build up and encourage or to degrade and condemn. There is great blessing when a name is called for purposes of upbuilding, encouragement, blessing, and prophecy. We have multiple opportunities every day to attach such edifying words and attitudes when we call out another person's name.

CALLING OUT OTHER NAMES

The power of calling out a name goes beyond human interactions. Some non-human living creatures can understand human words. A dog can learn his name and understand the tone of your voice when you call his name. My dog knows her name. When I say "Nelly," she directs her attention to me – usually! Some other animals can understand words and respond to a name. Among them are cats, horses, donkeys, deer, elephants, birds, pigs, rats and dolphins. These are beings with abilities to hear and respond.

Jesus instructed believers to speak also to non-human objects such as a mountain or a sycamine tree. He said those who have faith will say to this mountain, "move from here to there," and it will obey.[1] He said those who believe will say to the sycamine tree, "be rooted up and planted in the sea," and it will obey.[2] In these scriptures the Word of God instructs believers to speak to things that do not have ears and have no capacity in themselves to understand, respond, or obey.

These words of Jesus weave together a great truth, but most believers have not understood or practiced it. Many Christians will ask God to move the mountain, but this is not what Jesus taught or demonstrated. Some may ask God in Jesus's Name to move a sycamine tree into the sea, but this is asking God to do something Jesus instructed us to do. He said we who believe will ourselves speak directly to the mountain. This truth involves calling the name of an object that cannot hear and understand, speaking to it as though it can hear and understand, and commanding it to do something.

How is this so? Why would Jesus tell His disciples to speak thus to a mountain or a tree? He was teaching them about increased faith. This faith Jesus taught is predicated on the position and authority of a believer. Just as the Centurion was under authority and in authority and was able to say to those in his battalion, "go, come, and do this or that," and they obeyed him, so Christian believers can speak to people and objects under their authority to move from here to there, and they will obey. The Centurion understood this simple and great truth about authority and obedience causing Jesus to marvel at his great faith. Faith and authority are closely linked in these scriptures. This kind of faith is expressed by calling out a name to preach the good news and move mountains. (See Matt. 8.5-13 and Luke 17.5-10).

Jesus also instructed us to preach the gospel to the whole creation.[3] The whole creation includes organic and inorganic things, things that can hear the good news and things that have no ears to hear, things that can outwardly respond and things that cannot show a response. Creation is waiting for the revealing of the sons of God and itself is groaning in travail while waiting to be set free from its bondage to decay and obtain the same glorious liberty of redemption.[4] The gospel is to be preached to the whole creation, to every name, to every noun describing a person, place, or thing.

Both blessing and edification flow out of the mouths of believers when calling forth these names and proclaiming the good news of the gospel. Objects and unseen powers are unable to show a human like response when their name is called, but the speaking of a name is nevertheless powerful. This power is given to us by God from the beginning when He brought all the living creatures to Adam to see what he would name them. Just as power went forth from God as He spoke creation into being by using names, so we, created in the image of God, speak with power when we call forth names to bring the good news of the gospel.

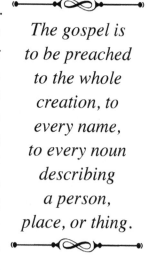

The gospel is to be preached to the whole creation, to every name, to every noun describing a person, place, or thing.

There are also names of beings in the unseen realm, of angels such as Gabriel and Michael, and for demons under the command of Satan (named Lucifer). Luke chapter 8 tells about an encounter Jesus had with a demonized man who lived by the tombs. Jesus had commanded the demons to leave the man. Then there was a brief exchange between Jesus and the demons. Jesus asked, "What is your name?" The answer was "Legion," for many demons had entered him.[5] In this power encounter Jesus used the power of calling out a name to drive out the demons from this man.

A believer who knows the realms of authority given by God can speak to those things as Jesus taught. Most Christians do not know the authority they have in the Name of Jesus Christ. Those who do know this authority in Christ may not use it much. This is a superficial discussion about this profound truth. See my book, "This Mountain," for much more commentary about these particular words of Jesus regarding faith and authority. "This Mountain" is written so we know and use wisely the authority given us in the Name of Jesus for His purposes and to advance His Kingdom. ("This Mountain," Xulon Press).

JESUS CALLED HIS DISCIPLES BY NAME

When we call out the name of another person, they will respond with diverting attention to you and take note of your attitudes and the circumstances with which you call their name. So simply calling out anyone's name in their hearing is powerful. There is an eternal, immeasurable blessing when Jesus, the Son of God, the Ancient of Days, the Alpha and the Omega, calls His own sheep by name and they follow Him.

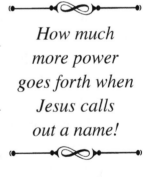

How much more power goes forth when Jesus calls out a name!

Jesus called His disciples by using their names. Luke records the following, "And when it was day, he called his disciples, and chose from them twelve, whom he named apostles; Simon, whom he named Peter, and Andrew his brother, and James and John, and

Philip, and Bartholomew, and Matthew, and Thomas, and James the son of Alphaeus, and Simon who was called the Zealot, and Judas the son of James, and Judas Iscariot, who became a traitor."[6]

Jesus called the twelve and named them as apostles. All twelve names are listed in the scriptures. Each one was called specifically by name. They responded by following Jesus as He led them. In the Good Shepherd analogy written in John 10, Jesus calls His own sheep by name.[7] This calling was extended to each of the twelve disciples and the same calling by name is extended to each of us.

Simon was the first one in the list of twelve disciples. He was also the only one in the twelve for whom Jesus gave a new name – Peter, which means rock. Jesus was intentional in giving Simon a new name. There was another Simon in the list of twelve apostles who was called the Zealot. Perhaps this nickname grew out of a need to distinguish between the two Simons, but another reason surfaces for why Simon Peter receives new name.

As Simon Peter followed after Jesus, the Holy Spirit gave him a revelation of who Jesus was. He was the Christ, the Son of the living God. When Peter spoke this truth about whom Jesus was and what His Name represents, then Jesus stated who Peter was. He was the rock (petra) on which He will build His church.

Peter, who received a new name from Jesus, who followed Jesus's calling, who received a revelation of who Jesus was, who spoke this insight to Jesus and the disciples around Him, and who received clarity from Jesus about the meaning of his given name for God's purposes in the church, was then given authority by Jesus to bind and loose. At the time when Jesus called Simon as His apostle, He gave a new name to him. He named him Peter (petra, which means rock) at his first calling. This name prophetically foretold of his role in establishing and governing the church.

The same process occurs for every believer who responds when Jesus calls them by name.[8] Here is the process:

30

1. Jesus calls you by name to follow Him.
2. You respond by calling upon the Name of Jesus and following Him.
3. The Holy Spirit gives you a revelation of who Jesus is.
4. You profess this revealed truth back to Jesus and to others.
5. Jesus then gives revelation by the Holy Spirit about who you are, your gifts, calling, and election.
6. Jesus gives you authority over certain areas as you carry out your part in the church, the body of Christ.

Note that Peter's identity was revealed to him AFTER he professed who Jesus was. The revelation of the Holy Spirit came first to Peter as to Jesus's identity, then to Peter as to his own identity. Peter did not receive insight about his calling and identity by introspection, taking some personality quiz, scoring some gifts assessment, or by some other aptitude inventory. It is the same for us. We get true understanding of who we are when we gain understanding by revelation of the Holy Spirit about who Jesus is and what He has accomplished for us.

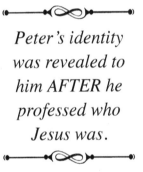

Peter's identity was revealed to him AFTER he professed who Jesus was.

SAUL OR PAUL

Jesus called Saul audibly by name in the midst of a bright light while traveling on the road to Damascus. Saul had been breathing threats and murder against the disciples of the Lord. He went to the high priest to get letters authorizing him to bring Christians bound to Jerusalem.

> Now as he journeyed he approached Damascus, and suddenly a light from heaven flashed about him. And he fell to the ground and heard a voice

> saying to him, "Saul, Saul, why do you persecute
> me?" And he said, "Who are you, Lord?" And he
> said, "I am Jesus, whom you are persecuting; but
> rise and enter the city, and you will be told what you
> are to do" (Acts 9.3-5).

When Saul persecuted Christians he was persecuting Jesus. Jesus did not say, "I am Jesus, and you are persecuting my followers." No, Saul was persecuting Jesus. To persecute Christians is to persecute Jesus. This is so because of the intimate, mutual identification between Jesus and His people. Jesus had said to His disciples, "You will be hated by all for my name's sake."[9] The church was now His body. To come against the church is to come against Jesus. Jesus was abiding in them and they were abiding in Him.[10]

Additionally we can conclude that Jesus's Name was upon the ones whom Saul was persecuting. His Name was put upon those believers. Just as God instructed Moses and Aaron to bless the people and in so doing God's Name was placed upon them, so Jesus is united with believers and His Name is similarly placed upon them. The epistle of James speaks of this matter in chapter 2: "Is it not the rich who oppress you, is it not they who drag you into court? Is it not they who blaspheme *that honorable name which was invoked over you*?" (James 2.6-7, italics mine).

Jesus called Saul (Paul) by name. Note the incredible power of Jesus's call. Saul's agenda was in every way against Christians and their message. "I myself was convinced that I ought to do many things in opposing the name of Jesus of Nazareth" (Acts 26.9). In this encounter he was thoroughly converted from his conspiring against Christians to become a Christian, joining with those he had opposed. This transformation happened when Jesus called his name twice. Saul was blinded by the light of Jesus's Name for three days.

God spoke to Ananias to go to Saul and lay hands on him to restore his sight. Take note of God's words to Ananias about Saul: "But the Lord said to him (Ananias), 'Go, for he is a chosen instrument of mine *to carry my name* before the Gentiles and kings and the sons of Israel; for I will show him how much *he must suffer for the sake of my name*'" (Acts 9.15-16, italics mine). Paul's calling was to carry Jesus's Name to Jews and Gentiles. It was the great and wonderful Name of Jesus that he was called to carry. This summarizes Paul's calling from God: to carry the Name of Jesus near and far.

Paul's conversion was so firmly established that he would now follow the One he was persecuting, despite knowledge of how much he must suffer for the sake of His Name. Note again the focus on the Name. God's words to Ananias did not say "how much he must suffer for my sake." It was "how much he must suffer for the sake of my name." It was Jesus calling Saul's name. Saul's repentance and conversion brought him to carry Jesus's Name and suffer for His Name.

Scripture does not include a passage in which God instructed Saul to be called Paul. Jesus called him Saul according to his current name. The name Paul is introduced at Acts 13.9. At that time the scripture states Saul was also called Paul. So it appears he had two names. But in the chronology of scripture there is a distinct change of Saul's name to Paul. After Acts 13.9 he is only known as Paul. Before this he was referred to as Saul. Also before Acts 13.9, when Saul and Barnabus are listed, Barnabus' name is listed first of the two names. After Acts 13.9 Paul's name is always listed first, ahead of Barnabus.

It is unclear how and why Saul's name was changed to Paul. Theologians have postulated several explanations but have not reached a consensus. Perhaps all of them have merit and contribute to the name Paul for this Apostle. Here are some explanations:

1. The meaning of these names. Saul means wanton, desired, or desiring. Paul means little or humble. He was no longer desiring as he was filled with the fullness of God (Eph. 3.19) and he was identifying with his humility before God and others. Paul wrote to the Corinthians: "For I am the least of the apostles, unfit to be called an apostle, because I persecuted the church of God" (1 Cor. 15.9).

2. It was customary then for Jews to have two names, one was Jewish and used among believers, and one Gentile name used among non-Jews. A change of name can occur when crossing into a different language or culture. For example, Piotr is a Russian name and Peter is English. Jorge is a Spanish name and George is English. Saul is a Jewish name and Paul is a Roman name.

3. A new name expresses a new nature. Paul is done with his old nature. He has been crucified with Christ. It is no longer he who lives but Christ who lives in him (Gal. 2.20). Paul is also his only recorded name from the time he throws himself into public ministry.

4. The name Paul notably occurs after his first convert who was named Sergius Paulus.[11]

Jesus continues to call people unto Him, to become His disciples. Do you hear this call? Can you perceive His speaking your name to invite you to a faith relationship with Him? When Jesus calls His sheep by name to lead them out, a great power goes forth to penetrate through all manner of sins, of disappointments, of regrets, and misunderstandings to speak directly to the innermost being. It comes as a knocking on the door of your heart and the calling of your name as He waits for you to open the door to Him.

ZACCHEAUS

The account of Zacchaeus is another testament to the power when Jesus calls by name. Zaccheaus was the short man who climbed up a tree in order to see Jesus. When Jesus saw him in the tree He called out the name Zacchaeus. How is it that this tax collector decided to give half of his possessions to the poor and repay anyone he had shorted by four-fold? What force could move him to reverse his pattern of collecting to one of multiplied repayment? It was because Jesus called him by name and visited him at his house.

Zacchaeus was a chief tax collector, but there is no evidence Jesus knew who he was prior to this encounter. It could be that Jesus spoke his name because He knew of him by natural means, that is, perhaps his disciples may have told him his name. But knowledge of Zacchaeus's name may have come to Jesus by supernatural means. Zacchaeus's profound repentance seems to indicate that his name was revealed to Jesus by word of knowledge from the Spirit of God. This inspired knowing of his name would itself garner his attention.

Imagine being part of a large crowd gathered to see a football game. The quarterback, whom you have never met, takes a time-out and runs to the sidelines and points you out in the crowd. He then calls your name and says, "Let's get a bite to eat after the game." It was this kind of calling that Jesus extended to Zacchaeus. This calling was all the more powerful as his name was spoken by the Son of God who was from eternity and was with God as the Word of God during creation. This Jesus powerfully called him by name and he repented and believed.[12]

Likewise Jesus calls you by name. When you respond to Him with repentance and faith, He brings you to a relationship with the Father God through Jesus by the Holy Spirit's power. Those who abide and remain in this relationship, to those who conquer because of the enduring relationship with the Father through Jesus, they are given a new name that is recorded in the book of life. The Spirit instructed John to write to the church at Pergamum: "To him who conquers I will give some of the hidden manna, and I will give him a white stone, with a new name written on the stone which no one knows except him who receives it."[13]

GOD PUTS HIS NAME ON PEOPLE

After God gave Moses the Ten Commandments, He sent an angel to guard and guide him. Look at what God said to Moses about this angel.

> Behold, I send an angel before you, to guard you on the way and to bring you to the place which I have prepared. Give heed to him and hearken to his voice, do not rebel against him, for he will not pardon your transgression; for *My Name is in him* (Ex. 23.20-21, emphasis mine).

God's Name was in this angel. God put His Name in that angelic being. He was therefore authorized by God to speak and act on His behalf. God commissioned that angel for His purposes by putting His Name in him. In the same way, God puts His Name on people whom He calls.

When God calls by name, those who respond with repentance and faith will receive forgiveness, blessings, and immeasurable inheritance. These benefits come through His Name.

A familiar and oft quoted blessing that God instructed Moses and Aaron to speak over the people was the means by which God put His Name on His people. This blessing was the means by which God put His Name on the people. When this blessing is quoted nowadays the last sentence of what God said to Moses is not included. These words to Moses came directly from God so all of them are important.

The Lord said to Moses, "Say to Aaron and his sons,
Thus you shall bless the people of Israel: you shall
say to them, The Lord bless you and keep you: The
Lord make his face to shine upon you, and be gracious to you: The Lord lift up his countenance upon
you, and give you peace. *So shall they put my name
upon the people of Israel*, and I will bless them"
(Num. 6.22-27, Italics mine).

The blessing spoken over the people was intended for the purpose of putting God's Name upon His people. God had Aaron
and his sons put God's Name upon the people. The blessing itself
accomplished this naming; and the placing of The Name brought
the blessings. Additionally, God's people, who had the Name of
God upon themselves and continued to walk under the authority of
that Name, remained under the ongoing blessings of God.

The Name of God remained upon His people whether or not
they remained true to His Name. If any of God's people called by
His Name should disregard and turn away from Him, His Name
remains with them, but the blessings to them and their land and
possessions may not continue. So we see God's persistent call to
His people to return to Him. "If my people WHO ARE CALLED
BY MY NAME humble themselves, and pray and seek my face,
and turn from their wicked ways, then I will hear from heaven,
and will forgive their sin and heal their land" (2 Chron. 7.14, cap-
itals mine).

This is another rather well known scripture verse where we
may easily pass over the prepositional phrase "who are called by
my name" and not recognize its importance. It would have been
enough for God to say 'If my people humble themselves..., but He
added the power of His Name that calls His people. He was then,
and is yet today, calling His people who have His Name upon them.

37

This same blessing, with the placing of God's Name on people, occurs at baptism. The spoken words that accompany the person encountering the waters of baptism include the Name of the Lord. You will hear the words, "I baptize you into the NAME of the Father and of the Son and of the Holy Spirit." Believers are baptized into the Name of the Lord Jesus. When Jesus's Name is so "put" upon believers in the sacrament of baptism, a covenant is established between God and the one baptized whereby the seal of the Holy Spirit, which is the guarantee of inheritance until possession of it, is acquired.[14]

Here again is the focus on the Name. Baptism could just as well be done in the Father, Son, and Holy Spirit. The words spoken at baptism could simply state, "I baptize you into the Father, the Son, and the Holy Spirit." The Name is included because the Name is a seal, a stamp upon the one being baptized, because the Name has special meaning and power as we are unpacking in this book.

> Acts 2.38: And Peter said to them, "Repent, and baptized every one of you in the name of Jesus Christ for the forgiveness of your sins; and you shall receive the gift of the Holy Spirit.

> Acts 8.16: ...for it (the Holy Spirit) had not yet fallen on any of them, but they had only been baptized in the name of the Lord Jesus.

> Acts 10.48: And he commanded them to be baptized in the name of Jesus Christ.

> Acts 19.5: On hearing this, they were baptized in the name of the Lord Jesus.

Eph.1.13-14: In him you also, who have heard the word of truth, the gospel of your salvation, and have believed in him, were sealed with the promised Holy Spirit, which is the guarantee of our inheritance until we acquire possession of it, to the praise of his glory.

CALLING ON THE NAME OF JESUS

Jesus calls His sheep by name and He leads them out and they follow Him. His calling comes to us, but we can also call on Him. We do so by calling on His Name. If a friend or even an enemy will turn to you when you call their names, how much more will the Lord Jesus Christ respond to those who seek Him and call His Name. Whoever does so with a sincere heart will be saved. Is this not also great power? Every human has the freedom to speak the Name of Jesus. When this comes from a humble heart that honors Him as Savior and Lord, there is power to become children of God and to gain access to the Father who is seated on the throne of grace. "And it shall be that whoever calls on the name of the Lord shall be saved."[15] "For, 'everyone who calls upon the name of the Lord will be saved.'"[16]

Once again these scriptures do not simply say "call upon the Lord." Instead, it states "call upon the NAME of the Lord." Certainly anyone who calls upon the Lord has the same access to Him. But the scriptures tell us to call upon the Name of the Lord. When Paul wrote his first letter to the Corinthians he begins by stressing this great truth which pertains to all people in all places. Paul's letter to the Corinthians was addressed to all those who in every place (not just in Corinth) call on the NAME of our Lord Jesus Christ.

To the church of God which is at Corinth, to those
sanctified in Christ Jesus, called to be saints together
with all those who in every place call on the name
of our Lord Jesus Christ, both their Lord and ours
(1 Cor. 1.2).

Matthew records two different accounts of two blind men
calling out to Jesus. In both records the blind men address Jesus
as the Son of David. This was the Name that all four blind men in
the two episodes chose to use. They apparently knew of Jesus heritage and probably the prophecies regarding the coming Messiah
who was now before them. They did not call Him Rabbi or Master
or Teacher. They said, "Have mercy on us, Son of David."[17] The
use of this name hearkened to Jesus's earthly lineage and the prophetic description of the Messiah who would come as a root of
Jesse. There was faith evident in these blind men as they chose to
call Him "Son of David." Perhaps they did not yet know His given
Name and be able to call Him Jesus. They did recognize that Jesus
came from the lineage of David and understood Him as the fulfillment of prophetic promises. These blind men were all healed of
blindness as they called upon the Son of David for mercy.

SECTION TWO

NAMES FOR GOD

In the last section we explored the meaning, purpose, and power of a name. This next section is devoted to understanding some of the nature of God by considering His Names. Just as a person's identity is connected to a name, so it is with God whose Name is revealed in the Word of God.

Chapter 5

NAMES FOR GOD

Then Moses said to God, "If I come to the people of Israel and say to them, 'The God of your fathers has sent me to you,' and they ask me, 'What is his name?' what shall I say to them?" God said to Moses, "I AM WHO I AM." And he said, "Say this to the people of Israel, 'I AM has sent me to you.'" God also said to Moses, "Say this to the people of Israel, 'The Lord, the God of your fathers, the God of Abraham, the God of Isaac, and the God of Jacob, has sent me to you': this is my name for ever, and thus I am to be remembered throughout all generations" (Ex. 3.13-15).

A FOREVER NAME

Moses knew the importance of a name and that the Hebrew people would ask for a name for God. It was not enough for them that God would be known as the God of their fathers. The people wanted to attach a name to these references and memories. Certainly God knew of this human need to know His Name as He created humans this way.

God knew what Moses was asking as it is God's nature to name things. So God said to Moses that His Name was "I AM THAT I AM." That is to say, God's nature cannot be confined to words or conceived by human thought. God's whole nature is implied in His existence, in His being, I AM WHO I AM. He exists as nothing else does. "I am the Lord, and there is no other."[1] His Name, I AM WHO I AM, signifies an eternal now, with which time has nothing to do. God exists outside of time.

God's Name, I AM, signifies an unconditioned existence independent from all other existence. All other existence is dependent upon "I AM." He is self-existent and has no dependence on any other. So He is self-sufficient and all sufficient, an inexhaustible reservoir of being which is eternal and unchangeable, the same yesterday, today, and forever. I AM THAT I AM is the kind of name that has no restrictions on God's identity and character.

This Name encompasses His omnipresence, omniscience, and omnipotence.

A PLURAL NAME

The words "lord" and "god" are not specific names as there were and are many lords and gods. The Hebrew words for the one Lord God are "Elohim", "Jehovah" (YHWH or Yahweh), and "Adonai." El or Elohim is Hebrew for God. Jehovah translates as Lord. Jehovah Elohim is the Lord God. Adonai is another Hebrew word for God. Adonai is the plural of Adon meaning Lord, Master, Father, and Owner.

In Hebrew, the ending "-im" normally indicates a masculine plural. However, when referring to the Hebrew God, Elohim is usually understood to be grammatically singular, a plural noun that governs a singular verb or adjective. Adonai and Elohim are plural forms of Adon and El respectively. However, these plural forms,

Adonai and Elohim, are both usually used with singular verbs and modifiers. In English this would be like saying, "They is happy" or "Horses runs fast." This does not fit our English language rules, but in Hebrew this is a normal usage of these words referring to the Lord God and is best understood as an emphatic plural or a majestic plural.

God began creation by speaking words that included names. "God called the light Day, and the darkness he called Night."[2] On the sixth day when God created humans, there was a change in the words God used to speak forth creation. In previous days of creation God said, "Let there be..." When creating humans, Gen. 1.26 says: And God said, "Let US make man in OUR image, after OUR likeness." There are a few other scriptures where God refers to Himself with plural pronouns (Gen. 3.22, 11.7, and Is. 6.8).

Scripture clearly establishes God as the one true God. Deut. 6.4 says the Lord is one. We know from the witness of scripture that He is three in one, the triune God. Adonai and Elohim are in plural form for emphasis and majesty, but may also refer to the Trinity - the Father, the Son, and the Holy Spirit, which was revealed through the incarnation of Jesus Christ.

The plural usage in this verse is not likely indicating that God consulted with other beings, such as the host of heaven's angels, when He made man. It may be a germ of truth about the Triune nature of God which is progressively revealed through scripture.

The Old Testament cites numerous references to the Spirit of God. For example, the Spirit of God was moving over the face of the waters at the beginning of creation.[3] With the coming of Jesus, there was much more revelation of the Father God, His One and only Son, and the Holy Spirit which is now given to all believers. John 1.1-3 says "In the beginning was the Word, and the Word was with God, and the Word was God. He was in the beginning with God; all things were made through him, and without him was not anything made that was made." Jesus, the Word of God, was with

God before creation. Creation came through Jesus, the Word of God. The witness of scripture in Genesis and John's gospel speaks of the Trinity.[4] Hence the inspired words of Gen. 1.26: "Let us make man in our image."

JESUS REFERS TO HIMSELF AS I AM.

Jesus used God's Name, which was given to Moses, when referring to Himself. Jesus is quoted in the Gospel of John as using the Greek translation of "I AM." He was likely speaking in Hebrew or Aramaic at the time. The written quote in the scriptures in Greek is obviously not in the same Hebrew words God used to speak to Moses. Nevertheless, the Word of God as recorded in the Gospel of John has Jesus referring to Himself as I AM.

The Jews had trouble with this as they would not even speak God's Name. They regarded it as too holy to speak. They also had a problem with Jesus using God's Name to refer to Himself. They knew Him as the carpenter's son. Some may have thought of Him as the Messiah who would restore Israel. They did not know Him as the Christ, God's Son, God Himself incarnate in human form. Jesus uses the reference "I AM" to hearken to scriptures familiar to the Jews. They knew God's Name was "I AM," "I AM WHO I AM."

Jesus calls Himself "I AM" in three instances in John's gospel. One instance occurs when Jesus converses with the Samaritan woman at the well. Jesus spoke to the Samaritan woman to reveal Himself as the Messiah. Jesus said to her, "I who speak to you am he."[5] In this conversation Jesus says "I AM." The Greek words for "I AM" are "ego eimi" (εγο ειμι). The Greek sentence structure for this verse is transliterated as "I AM, who is speaking to you." (ε γο ειμι, ο λαλων σοι.) Jesus uses "I AM" to describe Himself as one with God.

The second setting is recorded later in John chapter 8. Jesus referred to His eternal being with the Father God when He answered the Jews questions about who He was. In this setting He says "I AM" three times in His dialogue with the Jews.

> I told you that you would die in your sins, for you will die in your sins unless you believe that I am he (John 8.24, "I am he" is "εγο ειμι" I AM).

> So Jesus said, "When you have lifted up the Son of man, then you will know that I am he" (John 8.28, "I am he" is "εγο ειμι" I AM).

> "Your father Abraham rejoiced that he was to see my day; he saw it and was glad." The Jews then said to him, "You are not yet fifty years old, and have you seen Abraham?" Jesus said to them, "Truly, truly, I say to you, before Abraham was, I am" (John 8.56-58).

Jesus makes strong reference here regarding Himself as "I AM," just as God gave His Name to Moses. The statement therefore is not that Christ came into existence before Abraham did, but that He never came into being at all, but existed before Abraham had a being; in other words, He existed before creation, eternally, outside of creation as stated in John 1.1: "In the beginning was the Word, and the Word was with God, and the Word was God."

THERE IS POWER IN I AM

John's gospel describes a third moment where Jesus says "I AM." Judas brought a band of soldiers and some Jewish officers to arrest Jesus. Jesus came forward to them and asked, "Whom do you seek?" They answered Him saying they were seeking Jesus of Nazareth. Jesus then said, "I AM." This gets translated to English as "I am He." The Greek text says only "I AM" (ego eimi, εγο ειμι) just as God said His Name was when speaking to Moses.

When Jesus said "I AM" to these Jewish officers and the soldiers carrying weapons, they all drew back and fell to the ground. Here was a large group of armed men coming to arrest Jesus, who was alone except for the disciples with Him. Jesus steps up to meet these people coming to arrest Him. Certainly the soldiers were there to make a show of force. Jesus says "I AM" and they all fell backward to the ground. We can picture the situational irony as Jesus simply stood there and waited while these armed soldiers regained strength and arose to regroup and then arrest Him. The soldiers and their weapons were rendered powerless by the Name. Jesus's words, "I AM," caused those who were coming to arrest Him to lose their strength and fall to the ground.

> So Judas, procuring a band of soldiers and some officers from the chief priests and the Pharisees, went there with lanterns and torches and weapons. Then Jesus, knowing all that was about to befall him, came forward and said to them, "Whom do you seek?" They answered him, "Jesus of Nazareth." Jesus said to them, "I am he." Judas, who betrayed him, was standing with them. When he said to them, "I am he," they drew back and fell to the ground (John 18.3-6).

I AM SAYINGS IN JOHN'S GOSPEL

The Gospel according to John presents seven other "I AM" sayings of Jesus. Each of these use the Greek words for I AM, ego eimi (εγο ειμι). These usages of I AM are used by Jesus to describe to others who He is. These passages in John's gospel do not quote Jesus as simply saying I AM. Rather they are a more normal usage of a first person singular state of being. We might frequently say things like, "I am hungry," "I am a student," "I am a teacher" to describe ourselves in various ways. Jesus said, "I AM the …." These have an antecedent that describes who He is and what He does. Each I AM is followed by the definite article "the". Jesus is THE… meaning He is the paramount and supreme example of each I AM saying.

I am the bread of life 6.35, 48.

I am the light of the world 8.12.

I am the door of the sheep 10.7, 10.9.

I am the good shepherd 10.11.

I am the resurrection and the life 11.25.

I am the way, the truth, the life 14.6.

I am the true vine 15.1, 5.

Each of these seven I AM sayings of Jesus brings revelation about who He is. Each one begins with ego eimi – I AM. Jesus is saying I AM, making reference in these sayings to His Father's Name, I AM WHO I AM.

DESCRIPTIVE NAMES FOR GOD

As God's identity, character, and attributes became known to His people, certain descriptors were attached to His Name. These are scriptural Names for God that reveal His nature and indicate His unchanging will and actions. God is so wonderfully multifaceted that He has many Names that communicate some of His capabilities and character. To list just a few, He is:

Jehovah Jireh (The Lord Will Provide) Gen. 22.14.

El-Shaddai (The Almighty God) Gen. 17.1, 28.3, 35.11, 43.14, 48.3.

Jehovah Shalom (The Lord is Peace) Judg. 6.24.

Jehovah Shammah (The Lord Who is Present) Ex. 48.35.

El Elyon (The Most High God) Gen. 14.18, 19, 20, 22, Ps. 57.2, 78.35.

Jehovah Nissi (The Lord My Banner) Ex. 17.15.

Jehovah-Raah (The Lord My Shepherd) Gen. 48.15, 49.24, Ps. 23.1, 80.1.

Jehovah Rapha (The Lord who Heals) Ex. 15.26.

Jehovah Tsidkenu (The Lord Our Righteousness) Jer. 23.6, 33.16.

Jehovah Mekoddishkem (The Lord Who Sanctifies You) Ex. 31.13, Lev. 20.8.

El Olam (The Everlasting God) Gen. 21.33, Jer. 10.10, Is. 26.4.

Jehovah Sabaoth (The Lord of Hosts) 1 Sam. 1.3, Ps. 24.9-10, 84.3, Is. 6.5.

Qanna (Jealous) Ex. 20.5, 34.14, Deut. 4.24, 5.9, 6.15.[6]

These descriptive names for God are also characteristic of Jesus as Jesus is one with God. The Name of Jesus carries all of these attributes. Using Jesus's Name in prayer and ministry ascribes to all of these truths. We "run into" His Name by seeking refuge in His words and His being, by calling out His Name in prayer, by living and doing everything in the Name of Jesus, by denying self, taking up our cross, and following Him.

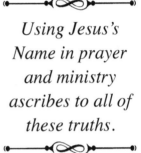

Using Jesus's Name in prayer and ministry ascribes to all of these truths.

RUN INTO THE NAME

Solomon wrote about the Name of the Lord, saying "The name of the Lord is a strong tower, the righteous man runs into it and is safe."[7] The NAME of the Lord is strong because the Lord God Himself is strong. The writer of this proverb could have written, "The Lord is a strong tower, the righteous man runs into it/him and is safe." This, of course, is true. The Lord is a strong tower to run to. He is absolutely the strongest tower. This proverb states the Lord's NAME is the One that is safe and strong, and the righteous should run into IT, that is, run into His tower, His Name.

Why would Solomon speak thus about the Name of the Lord? Why is there such focus on the Name? Because His Name is given to us to use. We "run into" the Name of the Lord when we properly use His Name. Here there is strength and safety.

Jesus "ran into" His Father's Name when He said, "I AM," to Judas and the band of soldiers who came to arrest Him. There was great power in voicing His Father's Name because Jesus "ran into" His Father. That is to say, Jesus had set aside His own will and resolved to do only His Father's will. "Not my will, but Thine, be done."[8]

Chapter 6

ETERNAL NOW – I AM WHO I AM

God's Name is "I am who I am." His Name is always present tense. God did not say, "I was who I was" or "I will be who I will be" or "I will be who I was." He said "I AM." God exists outside of time as He created time. So the Name "I AM" comprehends all times, past, present and future. He is the Eternal Now. Everything and every time is NOW for God. He is the One who was, and is, and is to come.[1] He is past, present, and future all at once because He is I AM, the Eternal Now. He lives outside of time and therefore cannot be constrained by time. "For with the Lord, one day is as a thousand years and a thousand years is as one day."[2] Let's look closer at the concept of time in an effort to understand God as "I AM."

> *Everything and every time is NOW for God.*

OUR TIME CONSTRAINTS

Time had a beginning and will have an end. We are living in the middle, between the beginning and the end of time. We are born into a time system which God established in creating our earth's rotation and revolution around the sun. In this world we cannot escape the progression of time, as it is a constant ticking of each passing second, minute, day, and year. Time is constant to us because we live on the earth whose rotations and revolutions are constant. Because we live our whole lives within these definitions of time, thinking outside of time comes with great difficulty. We may experience some awareness of this when we cross time zones and need to adjust our clock. If you have ever crossed the International Date Line you undoubtedly entertained some questions and thoughts about how our time is defined by the earth's rotation. So for all earth dwelling creatures time is a constant, continual progression through days and years because we continue in a solar system with rotations and revolutions that are constant.

But time is not always constant. Time is actually related to variables such as speed or velocity. That is to say, time is different between two objects when one is moving and the other is not. Albert Einstein described this as time dilation: moving clocks are measured to tick more slowly than an observer's stationary clock.

THE LAW OF RELATIVITY

Einstein's law of relativity states that time decreases as velocity increases. In other words, as something travels faster and faster, its associated time perspective gets slower and slower, when compared to a fixed, unmoving object. This theory of relativity pertaining to speed and time has been repeatedly tested and proven true. Einstein's theory of relativity is no longer a theory, but a law of physics. This law of relativity accurately describes the universe God created.

So as an object increases in speed or velocity, the progression of its time decreases. When extrapolated to the limits of speed, time then approaches zero. So at the maximum speed attainable in the universe, the speed of light, time is zero. Stay with me on this discussion about physics as this will give insight into the Name of God and some of His greatness.

The amount of time it takes for us to see light coming from the nearest star is about five years. This distance of five light years is almost 30 trillion miles. (5 years x 365.25 days/year x 24 hours/

day x 60 minutes/hour x 60 seconds/minute x 186,000 miles/ sec=29,348,568,000,000 miles.) From our perspective that light from that star was emitted five years ago. It took five years for that light to arrive to us. The light we currently see from that star gives us a picture of the state of being of that star five years ago. We are seeing into its past. For stars much farther away, we are seeing the more distant past. The current estimated size of the universe is roughly 13.5 billion light years (79 billion trillion miles or 79,241,133,600,000,000,000,000 miles or 7.9×10^{22} miles). The light from the stars farthest away from us was emitted about 13.5 billion years ago. The photographs you see of these farthest stars and galaxies show those celestial bodies as they existed around 13 billion years ago. When you look into the sky at the stars, you are seeing their past existence.

This is from our perspective as the stationary object with light coming to us. But if somehow one could ride on a light beam from that star which is five light years away, the time it would take for that light to arrive is not five years. At the speed of light, time stops – it is zero. One riding on a light beam from a star five light years away (30 trillion miles) would arrive in zero time. If you could ride on a light beam from a star that is one million light years away from the earth, you would travel that distance in zero time. You would arrive at earth with no passage of time. This is hard for our minds to grasp as we are constantly living on the earth's time and everything we see is relative to us.

GOD IS LIGHT

Light, because of its speed and relative time dilation, has a quality that characterizes God Himself. At the speed of light, time is zero. So light is always in the now, always present. Light has an inherent "eternal now" quality. Light is the one component of God's creation that carries an "I AM" quality. The word of God states that God is light. "This is the message we have heard from him and proclaim to you, that God is light and in him there is no darkness at all."[3] God is light. Jesus also spoke of Himself, "I am the light of the world; he who follows me will not walk in darkness, but will have the light of life."[4]

Light has an inherent "eternal now" quality.

This truth about God, that He is light, is consistent with His Name, "I AM." God, who is "I AM WHO I AM," is the Eternal Now. He is always present – omnipresent. He is everywhere. He is in every place and present at all times. He is the beginning and the end, the Alpha and the Omega. With God a day is as a thousand years and a thousand years is as a day. He is able to be present with everyone at all of our times. Though undoubtedly millions of prayers are spoken to God at any given moment on earth, He hears each one individually as He is "I AM." He is Light. He is not constrained by time. He is the Eternal Now.

LIGHT AND DARKNESS

We use the terms light and darkness to illustrate and characterize many things beyond its physical attributes. These uses are also found in the Bible.

- In physics terms, light is the presence of photons; darkness is their absence.
- In morality terms, light refers to upright choices and living; deeds of darkness are evil doings.
- In relationship terms, walking in the light is to have fellowship with one another and with the Lord Jesus Christ; walking in darkness is discord, unforgiveness, or hatred of others. He who says he is in the light, but hates his brother, is in the darkness still.[5]
- In knowledge terms, light is insight and understanding; being in the dark is being uninformed and not knowing.

For example, we might say, "Shed some light on the situation" or "We're in the dark on this matter."

- In witness terms, we are to let our light shine and not hide it under a bushel.

In scripture the themes of light and darkness are most commonly used to describe a person's choices, deeds, and relationships. To walk in the light is to be enlightened, to love one another; to walk in darkness causes one to stumble, not knowing where he is going. Some scriptures regarding light are not specifically referring to choices and lifestyle. These may include the physical characteristics of visible light we are considering here. Below is what the Psalmist said about light and darkness:

> Such knowledge is too wonderful for me; it is high, I cannot obtain it. Whither shall I go from thy Spirit? Or whither shall I flee from thy presence? If I ascend to heaven, thou art there! If I make my bed in Sheol, thou are there! If I take the wings of the morning and dwell in the uttermost parts of the sea, even there thy hand shall lead me, and thy right hand shall hold me. If I say, "Let only darkness cover me, and the light about me be night," even the darkness is not dark to thee, the night is bright as the day; for darkness is as light with thee (Ps. 139.6-12).

UTTER DARKNESS.

Have you ever been outside in absolute darkness, void of the light from stars and the city? Sometimes the moon is rather bright casting shadows at night. This can cause trouble sleeping when the full moon shines into a bedroom window.

There was one night when I found myself walking on a familiar trail while in abject, complete darkness. I was working a summer job at a Bible camp in northern North Dakota near the Canada border. This was a place that was far from any city lights. That particular night there were dense clouds so there was no light from the moon and stars. My bed was in a cabin on a small island situated about fifty yards from the shoreline of the lake. I did not bring any light source with me as I started out along the winding trail toward the suspended walking bridge to the island. It was about ½ mile distance from the lodge to the cabin where I resided. It was a familiar trail so I set out without a flashlight or lantern, thinking there would be some ability to see.

After ambulating about a hundred yards, I could not see anything. I thought my eyes would adjust to the darkness, but there was no light anywhere. I could not depend on my vision at all. My eyes were wide open with my pupils completely dilated, yet I could not detect a photon of light. I thought about returning to the lodge, but for whatever reason I decided to continue down the winding path. My arms were held in front to feel any brush or trees so I would not take a hit to my face. By sense of touch or feeling, I was able to navigate this trail. I also relied upon listening for the sound of my feet as I needed to drag them on the gravel trail for additional guidance.

It was a cool evening. The moisture on the leaves and bushes made me wet as I depended on feeling them for direction. I wonder now what would have happened had I not found my way and groped in the darkness being lost. This is what a blind person regularly experiences.

I eventually found my way to the foot bridge to cross over to the island. At this point the trail was without gravel; it was just dirt. I could no longer rely on the sound of my feet on gravel. Thankfully there were no large open spaces but rather various trails through brush and trees so I could have an idea where I was and where I needed to go.

Spiritually we can think we are walking in the light, but instead be groping in the darkness. This is true self-deception: thinking one knows his way and can see the path, yet in fact is unaware and misguided with resultant stumbling and harmful consequences. 1 John states that if you say you walk in the light, but hate your brother, you are in the darkness still.[6]

God has created us with the amazing sense of vision. We can see the details, colors, shapes, and sizes of items both near and far. The wavelengths of light that comprise the visible spectrum give us beautiful images of God's creation that inspire worship. Amazingly, our eyes can detect a single photon of light from the visible light spectrum. In utter darkness we can decipher just one lumen from a great distance. So physical light always overrules darkness. Darkness cannot hide light. Light always pierces darkness.

> In the beginning was the Word, and the Word was with God, and the Word was God. He was in the beginning with God; all things were made through him, and without him was not anything made that was made. In him was life, and the life was the light of men. The light shines in the darkness, and the darkness has not overcome it (John 1.1-5).

So time and light are related to one another. Both come from God who created all things. He calls Himself "I AM WHO I AM" as He exists as the Eternal Now. His Son Jesus has the same identity. We see Father God when we understand and see who Jesus is. Jesus is the light who exists from the beginning.

ONCE AND FOR ALL TIME

How can something that happens at one time be present and effective for all time? We sometimes see how past choices and events may have present or future consequences. For example, if you spend all of your money on something today, you may not have money for food and shelter tomorrow. If a tornado destroys a home, this will cause a lasting change of circumstances going forward. Our memories of our past lessons learned inform our present day decisions. Our past failures are sometimes our best teacher to bring wisdom and guidance for today.

Though we cannot know the future with absolute certainty, it can be that something we believe will happen in the future can bring us to change our current course. A couple planning to marry sometime in the future will certainly make plans and choices at present day. Hearing a weather report may change your travel plans. A farmer plants his crops believing that there will be a harvest.

In the year 999 A.D. there were many who interpreted the scriptures to believe Jesus would return at the end of that millennium. Because of this belief, some people did not attend to their plans for food and shelter. They did not plant crops or store up resources for themselves. They neglected their chores and waited, hoping and expecting to see Christ's return. There were enough people believing this and so acting that there was an economical depression that resulted. The second coming of Jesus did not happen then. To their credit they were prepared for Jesus's coming, but not for their daily needs. We can and must prepare for the future. We should be prepared for Christ's return for this will happen at a time that no one will suspect. So the present can change the future and our belief of what is coming in the future can change the present.

But is it possible for a present day event to have impact on what has already happened in the past? Can something that happens now change the past? The past is a fixed record of events we cannot undo. Nothing we say or do changes history. What has happened has happened. Sometimes we try to correct the past or make restitution for what has happened. Other times we may try to reproduce something desirable that occurred in the past. Those with a gambling addiction can be driven by a memory of winning or trying to recover from losses. Church members sometimes have fond memories of past times, maybe a revival, or certain songs or hymns. So henceforth they are trying to reproduce these times and get back to the glory days. None of these efforts will change what has happened. We can attempt to shape our present and future lives, but we cannot go back to redo or relive the past.

But with God all things are possible. He is the Eternal Now, the "I AM WHO I AM" who is not bound by time. Jesus's death and resurrection was an event that happened at one time in the midst of all prior history and all future time. How can the one time occurrence of Jesus's death and resurrection accomplish salvation for all believers who lived before Him, all who lived at that time, and all who live afterwards? Those who trust in Jesus for salvation and eternal life must believe what happened about 2000 years ago has present and future meaning and consequences. We must recognize and understand this one-time event has consequences for eternity, for all who lived at His time and since then, AND for all who lived before His life on earth. Jesus life on this earth, His death, resurrection, and His ascension back to heaven with the Father accomplished victory for all creation over all time.

Paul stated that he was crucified with Christ. "I have been crucified with Christ; it is no longer I who live, but Christ who lives in me; and the life I now live in the flesh I live by faith in the Son of God, who loved me and gave himself for me."[7] Paul writes this well after Christ's death, linking his life with Jesus's death and resurrection, recognizing its forward reaching effects which are not bound by time. Again in Col. 2.20, Paul writes inspired by the Holy Spirit: "If with Christ you died to the elemental spirits of the universe, why do you live as if you still belonged to the world?" Here Paul applies these truths to all believers, saying any believer, henceforth throughout time, has died with Christ on the cross. Furthermore Paul writes in chapter 6 of his letter to the Romans.

"Do you not know that all of us who have been baptized into Christ Jesus were baptized into his death?
We were buried therefore with him by baptism into
death, so that as Christ was raised from the dead by
the glory of the Father, we too might walk in newness of life. For if we have been united with him in a
death like his, we shall certainly be united with him
in a resurrection like his. We know that our old self
was crucified with him so that the sinful body might
be destroyed, and we might no longer be enslaved
to sin. For he who has died is freed from sin. But if
we have died with Christ, we believe that we shall
also live with him" (Rom. 6.3-8).

Paul states a profound truth that links our present time with a
past event. Not only did Jesus die for our sins and pay the penalty
for us, we who believe also died with Him. The Eternal Now, the
"I AM," who was, and is, and is to come,
is outside of time. He is always present.
The death and resurrection of Jesus is
once and for all time and all people. So
believers who live at any time in the
span of history are connected to the
great event that happened once in time.
In Christ the penalty of our sins was paid
before we were born. In Christ, believers
are joined with Him and crucified with
Him in an event that occurred long
before we were born.

*Believers who
live at any time
in the span
of history are
connected to
the great event
that happened
once in time.*

Who died on the cross? Jesus did. Who else died on that cross
about 2000 years ago? All believers. You did. Now we consider
ourselves dead to sin and alive to God.

The Bible states clearly that Jesus's work on the cross and subsequent resurrection has forward reaching effects. Additionally, this one time event has backward reaching benefits. Look closely at Peter's words, inspired by the Holy Spirit, as is recorded in 1 Peter 3. Take note of the words in bold italics pertaining to time.

> For Christ also died for sins *once for all*, the righteous for the unrighteous, that he might bring us to God, being put to death in the flesh but made alive in the spirit; in which he went and preached to the spirits in prison, who *formerly* did not obey, when God's patience waited *in the days of Noah*, during the building of the ark, in which a few, that is, eight persons, were saved through water. Baptism, which corresponds to this, *now* saves you, not as a removal of dirt from the body but as an appeal to God for a clear conscience, through the resurrection of Jesus Christ, who has gone into heaven and is at the right hand of God, with angels, authorities, and powers subject to him (1 Pet. 3.18-22, bold italics mine).

How could Jesus go back in time to preach to imprisoned spirits who formerly did not obey? He can because He is the great "I AM," the One who was, and is, and is to come. He is not constrained by time as He is light. At the speed of light, time is zero. At His death and resurrection, because He was made alive in the spirit, He went backwards in time and forward in time, as we see time. For Jesus, it is all NOW. The past, present, and future is all NOW as He is Light, He is outside of time. His death and resurrection was once for all time and for all people.

Baptism corresponds to this truth. In the waters of baptism, believers are united with Christ's death and resurrection. This past event has future benefits and our present lives hearken backwards in time. So Jesus's death and resurrection had retroactive and proleptic effects. That is to say, His death and resurrection worked backward and forward. The one-time event of His death and resurrection was effective for all past, present, and future salvation.

TRANSCENDING TIME

John records a dialogue Jesus had with Jewish leaders. It was a discussion about them questioning who Jesus was. The Jews asked if Jesus was greater than their father Abraham. Jesus replies with

Jesus's death and resurrection had retroactive and proleptic effects.

a profound statement that incited anger among them to where they took up stones to kill Him. His answer describes the transcendence of time for both Abraham, the father of faith, and Jesus, the Son of God. "Your father Abraham rejoiced that he was to see my day; he saw it and was glad" (John 8.56). Abraham, from centuries earlier, who lived and died like all humans, saw Jesus day and rejoiced. Abraham was declared righteous because of his faith and therefore benefited from the retroactive effects of Jesus's death and resurrection. Abraham saw Jesus's day and was glad.

The dialogue continues: "The Jews then said to him, 'You are not yet fifty years old, and have you seen Abraham?' Jesus said to them, 'Truly, truly, I say to you, **before Abraham was, I am**'" (John 8.57-58, emphasis mine). This was blasphemy to the Jews because Jesus said, "I AM" (ego eimi, the Name for God). Furthermore, Jesus is saying He is the Eternal Now, who transcends time, the One who was, and is, and is to come. He existed before Abraham. He is the Word of God, present with God and present as God from the beginning of time and creation. He is light and as light time is zero. He is omnipresent. It takes no time for Him to be anywhere at any time. He is everywhere all the time as it takes no time to be present as He is light.

SCRIPTURES ABOUT LIGHT

Many verses in the Word of God speak of light and darkness, several being listed below. As you read them, consider the meanings of light in terms of witness, relationships, understanding and insight, morality, and its physical properties.

- Ex. 10.22-23: So Moses stretched out his hand toward heaven, and there was thick darkness in all the land of Egypt three days; they did not see one another, nor did any rise from his place for three days; but all the people of Israel had light where they dwelt.
- Ps. 18.28: Yea, thou dost light my lamp; the Lord my God lightens my darkness.
- Ps. 27.1: The Lord is my light and my salvation; whom shall I fear? The Lord is the stronghold of my life; of whom shall I be afraid?
- Ps. 36.9: For with thee is the fountain of life; in thy light do we see light.
- Ps. 43.3: Oh send out thy light and thy truth; let them lead me, let them bring me to thy holy hill and to thy dwelling!
- Ps. 112.4: Light rises in the darkness for the upright; the Lord is gracious, merciful, and righteous.
- Ps. 119.105: Thy word is a lamp to my feet and a light to my path.
- Ps. 119.130: The unfolding of thy words gives light; it imparts understanding to the simple.
- Matt. 4.16: The people who sat in darkness have seen a great light, and for those who sat in the region and shadow of death light has dawned.
- Matt. 5.14: You are the light of the world. A city set on a hill cannot be hid.

- Matt. 5.16: Let your light so shine before men, that they may see your good works and give glory to your Father who is in heaven.
- John 1.4: In him was life, and the life was the light of men.
- John 1.5: The light shines in the darkness, and the darkness has not overcome it.
- John 1.9: The true light that enlightens every man was coming into the world.
- John 3.20: For everyone who does evil hates the light, and does not come to the light, lest his deeds should be exposed.
- John 3.21: But he who does what is true comes to the light, that it may be clearly seen that his deeds have been wrought in God.
- John 8.12: Again Jesus spoke to them, saying, "I am the light of the world; he who follows me will not walk in darkness, but will have the light of life."
- John 9.5: As long as I am in the world, I am the light of the world.
- John 11.9-10: Jesus answered, "Are there not twelve hours in the day? If anyone walks in the day, he does not stumble, because he sees the light of this world. But if anyone walks in the night, he stumbles, because the light is not in him.
- John 12.35: Jesus said to them, "The light is with you for a little longer. Walk while you have the light, lest the darkness overtake you; he who walks in the darkness does not know where he goes.
- John 12.36: While you have the light, believe in the light, that you may become sons of light." When Jesus had said this, he departed and hid himself from them.
- John 12.46: I have come as light into the world, that whoever believes in me may not remain in darkness.
- 2 Cor. 11.14: And no wonder, for even Satan disguises himself as an angel of light.

- 1 Pet. 2.9: But you are a chosen race, a royal priesthood, a holy nation, God's own people, that you may declare the wonderful deeds of him who called you out of darkness into his marvelous light.
- 1 John 2.9: He who says he is in the light and hates his brother is in the darkness still.
- 1 John 2.10: He who loves his brother abides in the light, and in it there is no cause for stumbling.
- Rev. 21.23: And the city has no need of sun or moon to shine upon it, for the glory of God is its light, and its lamp is the Lamb.

SECTION THREE

JESUS'S NAME

his third section builds upon the previous two sections by
focusing on the Name that is above every other name. The devil's scheme is to discredit, reduce, and malign the greatness and
power of the Name of Jesus. Some people choose to join in the
devil's plans. Nevertheless this Name is given to believers and carries great benefit. It is by His Name that the gift of salvation and
the appropriation of God's promises occur.

Chapter 7

IN VAIN

CURSING AND EVIL TALK

Cursing and foul language has become more and more common-place. Almost everywhere at any given time such speech can be heard. This is frequent and rampant in movies, on television, at sporting events and other social events. Why do people speak thus? What purpose does cursing and course language serve? It may seem to serve no purpose, rather the force of habit, in some people. Aware of this or not, such cursing, foul language, and especially taking the Lord's Name in vain is not without consequence.

Sometimes these words have a specific intent, and expression of humor, anger, or frustration. Vain words of cursing are also done for emphasis at making some point or to attempt to strengthen a statement or opinion that may otherwise be weak. If someone does not have enough substance to argue an issue or make an appropriate appeal, cursings and expletives are spoken instead. Name calling is often void of argumentative substance.

For some it becomes habitual, without much thought or care about what spews from the mouth. More and more cursing and coarse language, often with sexual references, is heard at work and even at home. Without restraint some parents speak obscenities in front of their children. Some children are belittled, chastised, and provoked with foul language spoken directly to them. These children will likely grow up to repeat what they have learned at home.

I am grateful I grew up in a home where there never was any kind of cursing or foul language. When a temptation might occur to blurt out something, there was not permission to speak wrongly. My parents taught this and demonstrated it consistently.

During summertime of middle school years a group of friends often gathered at the empty lot next door where we played various games throughout most of the day. The same manners were upheld among friends as we just "hung out" or played baseball, kick the can, football, and other games. Occasionally others from a different part of our small town of 2500 people came to join us at this lot. We always welcomed them. But whenever there was foul language they were told to stop such speech. The example and teaching from our homes spilled over to the playground and beyond. Nowadays it seems no one speaks up against such expletives, cursings, and taking the Lord's Name in vain.

At the Emergency Department where I work, sometimes patients come with cursing and shouting in anger. This is usually because life is not going the way they want and somehow they feel entitled to bring everyone nearby into their misery. Such language sometimes comes forth when a patient does not receive a prescription for a narcotic hoped for.

Along with loud cursing is increased violence, which is occurring in every Emergency Department. Most EDs have now hired security personnel to attend to safety and peace. In any other business such behavior would likely generate a restraining order or some refusal to serve in the future. Perhaps these people know that by law they cannot be turned away from an emergency room. Some are brought to us because of this kind of behavior which is demonstrated elsewhere out in the public.

Other patients sometimes decide cursing is acceptable because they are having pain. They permit themselves to speak this way despite no evidence that expletives and cursing provide any kind of relief. Not much thought is given about who may hear what is spewing from their mouths. Most of these same people, however, would guard their tongue when at a job interview or at some dignified event. It seems that some cannot get through any complete sentence they speak without adding cursing, swearing, expletives, condemnations, and name calling.

A DEFILED HEART

It is not what goes in our mouths that defiles us; it is what comes out of our mouths can defile us. Jesus states in Matt. 15.10-11, and 18: "And he called the people to him and said to them, 'Hear and understand: not what goes into the mouth defiles a man, but what comes out of the mouth, this defiles a man' ... But what comes out of the mouth proceeds from the heart, and this defiles a man." A tongue without a bridle, one who speaks without a filter, one who speaks in vain, is self-deceived. It stands in James 1.26: "If anyone thinks he is religious and does not bridle his tongue but deceives his heart, this man's religion is vain."

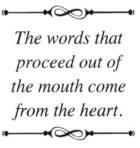

The words that proceed out of the mouth come from the heart.

The words that proceed out of the mouth come from the heart. We can understand what is in a person's heart by what is spoken by that person. We cannot regularly know what thoughts a person may have at any given time. The Word of God states that no one knows a person's thoughts except the spirit of that person.[1] Yet everyone can know what is in a person's heart by what that person speaks. "The good man out of the good treasure of his heart produces good, and the evil man out of his evil treasure produces evil; for out of the abundance of the heart his mouth speaks."[2] So when God's love is poured into a heart, the words that come from that mouth change radically to produce good.

AN UNTAMED TONGUE

Using foul language brings foul upon oneself. The ones who curse at their troubling circumstances bring more of the same upon themselves. Describing circumstances with profane words causes more troubling circumstances. Characterizing others with unwholesome words causes distrust and breakdown of relationships. The wisdom of Proverbs states in chapter 30, verse 32: "If you have been foolish, exalting yourself, or if you have been devising evil, put your hand on your mouth." To speak out such foolishness or evil designs causes defilement even before deeds are done. Put your hand on your mouth. Refuse to speak words that endorse or validate wrong thoughts and desires. Bridle the tongue that would speak curses on others or give false witness. Cease the use of profanities to describe unwanted circumstances. "Let there be no filthiness, nor silly talk, nor levity, which are not fitting, but instead let there be thanksgiving."[3]

Using foul language brings foul upon oneself.

Put your hand on your mouth to prevent speaking wrongly also about yourself. Do not bear false witness about yourself. Rather confess the truth of God's word, how God sees you and others through the atoning work of Jesus Christ. There is no condemnation for those who are in Christ Jesus. Despite this truth from God's Word, many take the accusations of the devil to heart and confess and profess untruths about themselves. Put your hand on your mouth and refuse to speak forth any falsities about yourself. Rather make the good confession about how God sees you as stated in His Word.

> So the tongue is a little member and boasts of great things. How great a forest is set ablaze by a small fire! And the tongue is a fire. The tongue is an

unrighteous world among our members, staining the whole body, setting on fire the cycle of nature, and set on fire by hell. For every kind of beast and bird, of reptile and sea creature, can be tamed and has been tamed by humankind, but no human being can tame the tongue – a restless evil, full of deadly poison. With it we bless the Lord and Father, and with it we curse men, who are made in the likeness of God. From the same mouth come blessing and cursing. My brethren, this ought not to be so (James 3.5-10).

From the same mouth can come both blessing and cursing. We are to bless and do not curse. "Bless those who persecute you; bless and do not curse."[4] The presence of God's love that is poured into the heart brings about blessing and good. "But I say to you that hear, Love your enemies, do good to those who hate you, bless those who curse you, pray for those who abuse you."[5]

We have the opportunity to impart grace to others and build one another up. Paul wrote in Eph. 4.29: "Let no evil talk (unwholesome word) come out of your mouths, but only such as is good for edifying, as fits the occasion, that it may impart grace to those who hear" (Parenthesis is from NIV). We have great power in our words to bless others, to call forth what God has deposited in others, and to encourage one another. The words of our mouths when combined with faith can say to a mountain, "Move from here to there," and it will obey and nothing will be impossible.[6]

TAKING THE LORD'S NAME IN VAIN

How frequently we hear our Lord's Name taken in vain! The wonderful Name of Jesus is sometimes also combined with other curses and expletives. To speak thus is to agree with the prince of this world who opposes and reviles the Lord and His people. The sons and daughters of disobedience speak as ones following the spirit of the world, even agreeing with the beast in the prophecy of John's Revelation who brought blasphemies against God. "And the beast was given a mouth uttering haughty and blasphemous words, and it was allowed to exercise authority for forty-two months; it opened its mouth to utter blasphemies against God, blaspheming his name and his dwelling, that is, those who dwell in heaven."[7]

We don't hear the names of the deities of other religions in such rants. No one cares to speak vainly of the names of Buddha, Hare Krishna, Mohammed, Hindu gods, etc. The primary goal of this evil spirit, the devil, is to blaspheme the Name of Jesus, to attempt to discredit the power in His Name. Those who take the Name of Jesus in vain are separated from His salvation and healing power.

Great blessing and power are given in the Name of Jesus to those who use His Name rightly; likewise, consequences come from its misuse. This warning of consequences comes with the third commandment: "You shall not take the name of the LORD your God in vain; for the LORD will not hold him guiltless who takes his name in vain."[8] The importance of the Lord's Name is preserved as one of the Ten Commandments. Those who speak God's Names vainly will not be held guiltless. Taking God's Names in vain causes separation from Him and invalidates prayers. Only by the Name of Jesus can we access the Father, as prayer in the Name of Jesus reaches the ears of the Almighty God. The third commandment is for our welfare as it preserves access to and relationship with God.

This commandment exists also to preserve the power and holiness of the Names of Father God, Jesus His Son, and the Holy Spirit. These Names of the Trinity are holy and powerful at all times and do not need a commandment to retain this dignity. This commandment is intended for us that we maintain our view of the holiness and power of the Lord's Name.

NOT ONLY WORDS

This commandment addresses any vain use of the Names of the Trinity. So taking the Name of the Lord in vain is more than just verbal cursing, it is misrepresentation of who He is. It is stating and living by lies about who God is and what is His purpose. It is misusing His Name, attaching the Name of Father, Son, and Holy Spirit to words, thoughts, actions that are contrary to His Word, His will, and His being.

Variations on God's Names are also commonly spoken. These "nicknames" may represent a vain use of God's Names. Examples are "Geez" or "Sheesh," which sound like a short form of Jesus. It is very common to hear the phrase "O my God" as a rather innocent exclamation about some remarkable events. When these words are spoken, it seems to me that most are not really calling on God in prayer. Is this a vain use of God's Name? I will let you decide your intentions if you use this phrase.

We are given His powerful Name to be used properly with honor, not vainly. This is the healthy fear of God that takes care to honor and revere His Names. Other expressions are without any hint of vain usage of His Names. Why not say, "Wow," "Awesome," "Interesting", or the all-purpose Norwegian word "Uffda"? Plenty of adjectives and explanations in any language available will not cause the guilty consequences which are warned about in the 3rd commandment.

GREAT WORKS DONE IN HIS NAME

Not everyone who says to me, "Lord, Lord," shall enter the kingdom of heaven, but he who does the will of my Father who is in heaven. On that day many will say to me, "Lord, Lord, did we not prophesy in your name, and cast out demons in your name, and do many mighty works in your name?"

And then will I declare to them, "I never knew you;
depart from me, you evildoers" (Matt. 7.21-23).

These remarkable words clearly state that doing such mighty works, including prophesying and casting out demons, when done by people who do not know the Lord and do not do the Father's will, is in fact evildoing. It is evil to use Jesus's Name without knowing Him and being known by Him, even if the works done are mighty with prophesying and casting out demons. It is evil if the use of that great Name is not operating from a relationship with Jesus and from obedience to the will of the Father. Jesus called any other use of His Name as evil. It is doing evil to perform mighty works in His Name without knowing Him and without obeying the will of the Father. Using the Name of Jesus properly must come from a relationship with Him where He knows you and you know Him. Out of this relationship comes obedience to the will of the Father in heaven.

Sadly there are those who wrongly extrapolate these verses to say ALL such works of prophesy and casting out demons are evil doings, even when coming from true disciples of Jesus who know Him, are known by Him, and who operate in the will of the Father. To make this conclusion overlooks the wonderful witness of scripture depicting Jesus and His disciples and the early church doing these works in Jesus's Name in the will of the Father to advance His kingdom.

SEVEN SONS OF SCEVA

In the Acts of the Apostles some men decided to use the Name of Jesus to attempt to exorcise someone who was demonized. They must have seen or heard about the power in the Name of Jesus to accomplish this. Perhaps they heard of or saw the Apostle Paul use the Name of Jesus in this way. So they spoke to the demon in the Name of Jesus who Paul preaches. The demons replied, "I know

Jesus and I know Paul, but who are you?" They turned to attack these seven sons of Sceva. They were unsuccessful in driving out the demons. Rather these seven left bleeding and naked as the demons took opportunity to attack them.

> Then some of the itinerant Jewish exorcists under-took to pronounce the name of the Lord Jesus over those who had evil spirits, saying, "I adjure you by the Jesus whom Paul preaches." Seven sons of a Jewish high priest name Sceva were doing this. But the evil spirit answered them, "Jesus I know, and Paul I know; but who are you?" And the man in whom the evil spirit was leaped on them, mastered all of them, and overpowered them, so that they fled out of that house naked and wounded. And this became known to all residents of Ephesus, both Jews and Greeks; and fear fell upon them all; and the name of the Lord Jesus was extolled. (Acts 19.13-17).

Though it was Christ's plan for this demonized person to be set free, they were misusing Jesus's Name. Jesus instructed His disciples to heal the sick, raise the dead, cleanse lepers, and cast out demons. Nevertheless these seven sons of Sceva were misusing Jesus's Name, not because of their intent to deliver the person from demonic forces, but because they did not know Jesus, His purpose, His word and will. They did not have the protective seal of the Holy Spirit over them so they were exposed and vulnerable to demonic forces that overpowered them.

"We know that anyone born of God does not sin, but He who was born of God keeps him, and the evil one does not touch him."[9] If you are born of God and sealed by the promised Holy Spirit, you have no need to fear the forces of the unseen world, for He who is in you is greater than he who is in the world.

The effective use of Jesus's Name comes from a relationship with Him based on trust and obedience to His Word. Those in such a relationship with Jesus are known in the unseen world. The demons knew Jesus and they knew Paul, but they did not know these sons of Sceva as they did not have this relationship with Jesus and authority to use His Name. The demons, principalities, and powers of this present darkness know those who rightly use Jesus's Name - and they tremble.

> John 14.23-24: Jesus answered him, "If a man loves me, he will keep my word, and my Father will love him, and we will come to him and make our home with him. He who does not love me does not keep my words; and the word which you hear is not mine but the Father's who sent me.

Like the Ark of the Covenant, when it was in the hands of the Philistines who did not honor and obey the Lord God, so that plagues came upon them, the Name of Jesus is powerful for those who know Him and submit to Him, but brings judgment upon those who do not. "He who believes in the Son has eternal life; he who does not obey the Son shall not see life, but the wrath of God rests upon him."[10]

The Name of Jesus is powerful for those who know Him and submit to Him, but brings judgment upon those who do not.

"MANY WILL COME IN MY NAME"

Using Jesus's Name in vain also includes ones who come with a message claiming they are acting and speaking on behalf of Jesus, but their message is comprised of empty words, deception, and/or licentiousness (permissiveness). As they present these ideas and proclaim their message, they attach the Name of Jesus to their words as a supposed endorsement from Him. Some go further to proclaim they have a special anointing from God, even claiming to be the Messiah or Christ Himself. "And he said, 'Take heed that you are not led astray; for many will come in my name, saying, "I am he!" and, "The time is at hand!" Do not go after them.'"[11] "For many will come in my name, saying, 'I am the Christ,' and they will lead many astray."[12]

"Many will come in my name, saying, 'I am *he*.'" (italics mine). The original Greek phrase here is "I am" (εγο ειμι). The pronoun "he" is not present in the Greek text. These who come deceptively and falsely in Jesus's Name do so saying the Name of God – ego eimi (εγο ειμι), I am. These pretenders are not sent by God. They actually come in their own name, are self-serving with selfish ambitions, but claim "I AM." Their message of licentiousness is enticing to many as it allows a permissive lifestyle, promising freedom, but they themselves are slaves of corruption.[13]

> But false prophets also arose among the people, just as there will be false teachers among you, who will secretly bring in destructive heresies, even denying the Master who bought them, bringing upon themselves swift destruction. And many will follow their licentiousness, and because of them the way of truth will be reviled. And in their greed they will exploit you with false words (2 Pet. 2.1-3a).

Chapter 8

REDUCING THE NAME

A THEOLOGY OF SUFFERING

Many great truths are revealed and explained through the cross of Christ. What happened on the cross is the pivotal event of all history that purchased salvation retroactively and proleptically. The cross is the atoning sacrifice as the Son of God took the sins of the world upon Himself and paid the penalties of sin once and for all generations and all time. The theology of the cross then becomes the lens through which all of scripture in viewed, the course upon which every believer should embark, and the interpretation of all of life's circumstances.

The cross of Christ is so profound because of the subsequent victorious resurrection from the dead. If there were no resurrection, Jesus's death on the cross would not be different from any other death sentence. There would be no such victory. The cross gains its meaning because there was resurrection.

The Christian faith is founded on both the cross and resurrection of Jesus Christ. However, some seem to embrace Jesus's way of the cross so closely so as to almost disregard or dismiss the victory of the resurrection. This is to glory in life's sufferings as an end itself, identifying more with Christ as the suffering servant than Christ as victor over sin, disease, death, and the devil. The power of the resurrection does bring believers to heaven, but it also signifies the Kingdom of God is near and brings heaven to earth. Some may embrace the cross of Jesus that finished everything in such a way that they stay in a place of suffering and defeat. They are holding to the words of Jesus, "It is finished", as though, since the time He spoke those words, He is finished with any further work on earth beyond forgiveness of sins and the gift of eternal life.

From this perspective, believers should then patiently suffer as Jesus did until they are taken to heaven. This is fueled by a belief that such is the way of suffering for a Christian who follows Jesus. To them, accepting all struggles, sickness, sins and pains is a fact of life, just as Paul knew that God's grace was sufficient for his thorn in the flesh.

Some seem to embrace Jesus's way of the cross so closely so as to almost disregard or dismiss the victory of the resurrection.

However, this perspective lacks the belief that heaven can come down to earth, that the Kingdom of God is near, or that the great promises of the scriptures might apply and be fulfilled in this life. So the pains of life are embraced as a way of identifying with Christ's sufferings. No prayer of deliverance or healing is offered to God because of a belief that no healing or deliverance will occur. The expected disappointment embraces a theology of suffering.

The Apostle Paul, who saw many miracles, also suffered greatly for the Name of Jesus. Paul did not derive his theology from his experiences, rather from the inspiration of the Holy Spirit. When he was discouraged he did not forsake the inspiration of the Holy Spirit and the truth of God's Word. Rather the Word of God and inspiration of the Holy Spirit informed and interpreted his experiences. He pressed through whatever disappointment he may have contended with at these times. He did not build his theology around any such discouragements. Paul experienced both great suffering and great miracles and he ministered under the great grace and mercy of the Name of Jesus. We can read of his great faith and understanding of God's will and purpose in the inspired Word of God that came through Paul's epistles.

A THEOLOGY OF DISAPPOINTMENT

> Hope deferred makes the heart sick, but a desire fulfilled is a tree of life. He who despises the word brings destruction on himself, but he who respects the commandment will be rewarded (Prov. 13.12-13).

We all know people close to us who died despite many prayers and supplications. I have prayed for healing for many who instead died of some type of disease. There is a time to die. For Christian believers this is a great blessing to go home to the Lord in heaven. But we all know ones who die young, who leave young children without a father or mother, or children who die before their parents. There are ones who die in old age and are ready to enter into their inheritance in heaven, but others have lives cut short by trauma, overdose, and disease.

Recently I turned on the car radio and came into the middle of a conversation between the talk show host and a man who was working to educate others about street drugs. He told the tragic story of how his only son died of a drug overdose. This father did not know his son was abusing drugs until his death from those drugs.

The host of the radio program asked this father if he goes to church and has faith in God. He replied he is no longer going to church. Up until his son's death, he had been attending church, but now he was not sure what to believe anymore. Though he did not specifically say it, he was clearly wondering how God could let this happen. There was some degree of blame or accountability that he ascribed to God in regard to his son's death. If this father believed God was in control then he could hold God responsible for letting his son die young.

It is common to hear professions of faith such as "everything happens for a reason" or "God is in control." This system of belief works nicely with a favorable outcome, but when tragedy or calamity comes along, what does this say about the goodness and power of God?

I do not find any scriptures stating God is in control. The Word of God states that He has all authority and all power. Nothing is impossible with God. He has given control to people who can chose to obey or disobey, yield to the Spirit or quench the Spirit, follow after or disregard the Word of God who created all beings and things. God is in charge, but not in control. He has given control to people. There will come a day when every knee will bow, in heaven and on earth and under the earth, and every tongue confess that Jesus is Lord. That day has not yet come. God is seated on the throne of the universe as King of kings and Lord of lords. He has not yet brought the new heavens and new earth in which righteousness and peace dwell.[1]

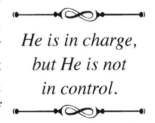

He is in charge, but He is not in control.

God allows bad things in this life because He has given control to people. He intervenes in answer to prayer. He is faithful to His promises. He has given control to people. Those who yield their lives to God through Jesus Christ, who call Him Lord thereby giving Him control, have access to His throne of grace and mercy to receive help in time of need. God is looking for such people that He can show His love and power. He is yearning jealously for the spirit He created in us and wants to bring life and peace.

People have freedom to make decisions and sometimes do things against God's will. This does not make God responsible. He is not to blame as He has given control to people who can in turn do what is either sinful or pleasing before God. It is a temptation of the devil to blame God for things He did not do.

Part of my Pastoral training included two months of chaplaincy work in a hospital. I noted during that time that every time I was called to the Emergency Department to give support to family members at times of tragic loss, those tragedies occurred because someone was choosing to break the law. There was speeding, alcohol abuse, hunting out of season and after hours, and other choices that contributed to tragic outcomes.

But not all such misfortunes occur because of wrong human choices. Forces of nature such as storms, hurricanes, tornadoes, earthquakes, fires, etc. cause great suffering. Other calamities occur apart from any wrongful human intentions. Jesus said trials and tribulations will come in this world, but He has overcome the world.[2] (John 16.33).

Trials and tribulations of this life become a test of faith. Questions come to us at these times. Do the great promises of scripture apply for now? Can Christians believe and trust in the promises of the Word of God to be active and working now, today, in this life? Virtually every believer has prayed for something or someone without receiving the desired request. Some of these prayers were clearly based on the promises of scripture and prayed in the Name of Jesus. Sooner or later it happens to all believers that we encounter such disappointments and discouragements. This becomes a vulnerable time for the believer whereby the devil may take opportunity to bring accusation and doubt.

At these times we are tempted to disregard or disbelieve some of the promises of scripture because they did not seem to work for us. We chose to believe the Word of God and prayed in the Name of Jesus, but nothing happened. At these times some may build a theology based on these disappointments. That is to say, when a believer learns of the great promises of scripture and asks the Father in Jesus's Name, but those prayers seem to go unanswered, an explanation in a person's beliefs is instituted to account for the disappointment. When God is asked to heal someone, but instead the person dies from the disease, this becomes a vulnerable time for testing our faith in the Word of God. We all have encountered these trials that serve to test our faith. Some conclude that at least some of these promises in the Word of God are not for now. Others entertain an attitude of betrayal by God.

When Martha and Mary met with Jesus, Mary sat with Jesus, but Martha was busy doing lots of work. Before long she came to Jesus expressing her disappointment saying, "Don't you care?"

Martha's encounter with Jesus did not go as she hoped or expected and it brought her to question Jesus's love and care for her. You can see Martha's belief that Jesus had betrayed her. Yet Martha did the right thing by bringing this directly to Jesus, being honest with Him, and leaving her work and drawing near to Him. Martha was troubled with many things, but Jesus said Mary had chosen what was better. So people have the choice to sit with Jesus as Mary did, and fellowship with Him and receive from Him; or they are free to choose to question Jesus's level of care because life did not occur as hoped and expected.[3]

At those times of disappointment we are faced with a choice: to press in all the more to the Lord and His Word; or choose to believe our experiences over against the eternal Word of God. Either we will bring our theology down to fit our experience or we will bring our experi- ence subject to the Word of God. Either

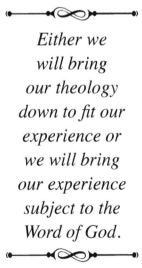

Either we will bring our theology down to fit our experience or we will bring our experience subject to the Word of God.

we will accept only the certain words of scripture that fit our lifestyle, beliefs, and experiences and disregard the others, or we will believe all scripture and expect our experiences and beliefs over time to become consistent with the Word of God in the Bible.

So to embrace only the sufferings, without hope for God's caring intervention, becomes in fact a theology of disappointment and discouragement that has chosen to give up on and disregard some or most of the great promises of God given us in the Name of Jesus. Such faith does secure salvation for eternity, which is no small matter, but this also effectively disregards the victory Jesus's won to bring heaven to earth in this age and time. Jesus taught us to pray, "Thy kingdom come, thy will be done, on earth as it is in heaven."

The Apostle Paul counted everything as loss in comparison to the surpassing worth of knowing Christ Jesus. He strove to know Christ and the power of His resurrection and to share in His sufferings becoming like Him in His death. He embraced both the cross and the resurrection. So in the Name of Jesus we are baptized into Christ's death in order that, being joined with Him in His death, we would also be united with Him in His resurrection, walk in newness of life, and no longer be enslaved to sin. Jesus taught us to pray that God's will be done here on earth as it is in heaven. To embrace the promises of the Word of God requires that we also embrace the process of faith. Jesus instructed His disciples to declare that the Kingdom of God is near. All of this is given to us in the beautiful, wonderful, and powerful Name of Jesus.

REDUCTIONIST THEOLOGY

The Name of Jesus meant more to the early church than it does to us, having an expectant benefit then that is not so often believed in these days. Today the wonderful, powerful Name of Jesus is stated in prayer and sung about in church, but for many there is little expectation that the workings of the Holy Spirit at the time of the early church, as recorded in the Acts of the Apostles, would occur today. We have not grasped the purpose and power of the Name. We have not understood how to properly use the Name of Jesus. We have not persisted in choosing to believe the eternal Word of God. We have instead resorted to believing our own temporal experiences. The Word of God then gets reduced to a philosophy and theology that sets aside some of the great promises bestowed to us in the Name of Jesus.

As a result of this process a reductionist theology evolves, that is, believing and acting on only the scriptures that seem to work or seem practical for today. Some profess that the Word of God in its entirety is true, but set aside some of the great promises as coming true as an inheritance of eternity and not for this life. So the Word of God is reduced to less than what is recorded in the scriptures.

Either we will develop a theology that fits our experiences or we will uphold the Word of God that informs, redeems, and shapes our experiences. Either we will ascribe to only those truths that seem to fit our culture and experiences and beliefs, or we will subject our beliefs and experiences to the eternal Word of God.

EDUCATION

Instead "Education" has taken place of the Name. Education in itself is good as we all need to grow up in our understanding of the world and the Word of the Lord. We are to be taught in Him, in Jesus, as the truth is in Jesus.[4] Paul states in Colossians that all the treasures of wisdom and knowledge are hid in Jesus Christ.[5]

But education can and has taken place of the Name of Jesus in many ways. Such education can be raised up against the knowledge of God. We hear this in society and in the church. In our culture, education is often touted as the way by which we can overcome societal ills. One can frequently hear in news reports how many problems can be attended to and remedied by education (usually without specifying what is the content of education to be delivered). The assumption is that all aspects of society would succeed and prosper if only there was better education. If fact, knowledge and education are more accessible now than any other time in history, yet the problems continue.

In the church, a Christian education class is presented as a way to grow in faith. Those who attend such didactic, classroom events are sometimes viewed as the more seasoned, pillars of the church, simply by attending or teaching such classroom studies. Though Jesus did teach, His strategy for discipleship was not classroom based, rather more like an apprenticeship whereby there was observation, then doing, then reflection and instruction, then more doing. Jesus's disciples observed Him doing the work of the ministry as He went about doing good, healing every disease, teaching in the synagogues, and preaching the gospel of the Kingdom of God. Then Jesus told them to do the same things they observed Jesus doing. They returned rejoicing as they saw the power of the kingdom of God displayed as they ministered in the Name of Jesus.

In many sermons and teachings, the dos and don'ts for moral living have supplanted the power of the Name of Jesus. The wisdom of men has taken the place of the power of God. Today we attempt mental miracles and sometimes state God's physical miracles are even purported as not necessary. One mighty miracle today in the Name of Jesus is worth more than the preaching of a hundred philosophical sermons. All too often the main point of preaching is to stir up Christians to do more good things and stop doing bad things. The focus is more on the doings of humans as if we are human doings instead of human beings. Misplaced is the understanding of and proclamation of the great Name of Jesus and what He has done for us. Also lacking is the recognition that apart from Christ we can do nothing.[6]

> See that no one makes a prey of you by philosophy
> and empty deceit, according to human tradition,
> according to the elemental spirits of the universe,
> and not according to Christ (Col. 2.8).

Chapter 9

DISCERN THE BODY

Like any other name that makes reference to a certain person, so the Name of Jesus is connected to His person, His body and blood. However, unlike any other person who ever lived, Jesus's body and blood has special benefits for all people for all time. His blood was shed for the sins of the world. A complete price was paid for every sin committed by every person who ever lived.

This grace is extended to all, but the benefit of this free gift is not complete until received by a believer. Like an inheritance never collected, a person can neglect or refuse this free gift. Like a Christmas present addressed to someone but is never opened, the provision is given but not received. He is the expiation for our sins, that is, He made provision for our forgiveness and salvation, but the appropriation of this free gift occurs when any sinner humbly approaches the throne of grace and calls upon the Name of Jesus. By the Name of Jesus we access His blood shed for us. There is no other name by which one can be saved. The blood of Jesus brings us to heaven as a free gift.

By His Name we actually access the whole person of Jesus, that is, His blood, His body, His soul, and His Spirit. Human beings are created with body, soul, and spirit. We can call upon another person's body, soul, and spirit by calling his name. Jesus was fully human and is fully Divine. He is God Incarnate, God made flesh.

91

So He is God's body, soul, and spirit. He gave His body, soul, spirit, and His blood on the cross as a sacrifice for us. By His Name we have access to all of Him. When we humbly and sincerely use the Name of Jesus, we invoke Him in Body, Soul, Spirit, and Blood. By His Name we have access to His blood for the forgiveness of sin, victory over the devil, and eternal life. By His Name we have access to His body for healing and wholeness of our bodies. By His Name we have access to His soul as He gives to the spiritual man the mind of Christ and the will to do His will. By His Name we have access to His Spirit as He prayed to the Father to send us the Holy Spirit to dwell in us and release power, gifts, fruits and counsel from that same Spirit.

Let's look specifically at calling Jesus's Name for accessing His body. His physical body served an eternal purpose as He was beaten and stricken. He was whipped and wounded for our healing. Because of Jesus's life, death, and resurrection, a complete price was paid for our healing and wholeness in body, soul, and spirit. This provision for healing was made for all people of all time, but the appropriation of this benefit is not automatic. Like opening a birthday gift or claiming an inheritance, access to the body of Christ and the healing benefits are attained by faith in Jesus and calling upon His Name. By the stripes of His *body* we are healed.[1] As the blood of Jesus brings believers to heaven, so the body of Jesus brings heaven to believers. Jesus's blood brings us to heaven and Jesus's body brings heaven to us.

THE LORD'S SUPPER

Paul wrote to the Corinthians about proper understanding of and use of the Lord's Supper. The Corinthian church needed correction as some were over-eating as though it were their meal for that day. These people ate without regard

Jesus's blood brings us to heaven and Jesus's body brings heaven to us.

for the others so that the bread and juice were consumed before all could partake. They were taking these elements as food and not aware of the great blessings and provisions in this sacrament. They did not consider the food and drink as a means of grace. Nor were they aware of the judgment that comes upon them when partaking of bread and cup in an unworthy manner. In this context Paul instructs them and us about the body and blood of Jesus and the meaning of the Lord's Supper.

> As often as you eat this bread and drink the cup, you proclaim the Lord's death until he comes. Whoever, therefore, eats the bread or drinks the cup of the Lord in an unworthy manner will be guilty of profaning the body and blood of the Lord. Let a man examine himself, and so eat of the bread and drink the cup. For anyone who eats and drinks without *discerning the body* eats and drinks judgment upon himself. That is why many of you are weak and ill, and some have died" (1 Cor. 11.26-30, italics mine).

Some believe they can never be worthy of the body and blood of the Lord and therefore abstain from partaking in the Lord's Supper. This is missing the message. In truth, no one in himself has a worthy standing before God. His grace is extended to us through His Son so that while not deserving and without any merit of our own we are welcomed to the Lord's table. By His Name everyone has confident access to His throne. This passage is not advising against partaking of the elements of the Eucharist. Paul is giving instruction regarding partaking in a worthy manner.

Note that Paul speaks of both the blood and the body of the Lord as these are the two components remembered in the Lord's Supper. Then he states anyone who eats and drinks without discerning just the body drinks judgment upon himself. Paul did not say "without discerning the body and the blood." In the setting of partaking in the body and blood, he spoke only of "discerning the body."

What is the message here? What is the meaning of this? What is it to discern the body? Is there no need to discern the blood? It is important to understand this as Paul informs us that many are weak and ill and some have died because they did not discern the body, bringing judgment upon themselves. Paul is offering wisdom here for health and well-being.

What is it to discern something? What is the body that is to be discerned? Why is there no statement about discerning the blood?

First, what does discern mean? To discern something is to distinguish, recognize, or understand. To discern is to make a right estimate of the character or quality of a thing. Other translations of the Greek word for discern (διακρινω - diakrino) use synonyms including honor, judge rightly, recognize, distinguish, or estimate aright. So to discern the body is to recognize, understand, honor, and judge rightly the body.

So what then is the body that is to be discerned? This has occupied ongoing discussion among theologians. Is it Christ's physical body; is it Christ's body, the church; or is it one's own physical body? The scripture does not give any modifiers to specify whose body is to be discerned.

I think all three have merit and give insight. To discern the body is to understand Christ's physical body, the church as the body of Christ, and one's own physical body. Believers are united with Christ and make up His body since Jesus ascended to heaven. We must understand (discern) this great truth that believers are crucified with Christ and now live in Him. Not only did Jesus die on the cross, every believer who calls on the Name of the Lord Jesus died with Him on that cross.[2] our bodies are united with His body in death and resurrection. Additionally, Christ's physical body was wounded, whipped, striped and stricken for us.

What is the body referring to in this passage? Jesus's physical body, but also the church, the body of Christ. Furthermore, it the physical body of every person who partakes of the Lord's Supper. Let's unpack these three so as to better understand this mystery and receive benefit, health, and provision through the work of Jesus on the cross.

CHRIST'S PHYSICAL BODY

To discern the body of Christ is to understand the benefits of the atonement from God to believers through His Son's physical body. If we look at the circumstances of Jesus's trial and sentencing only from a human perspective, we could conclude He was scourged and beaten because the religious leaders incited the crowds to release Barabbas and crucify Jesus. If we look at these same circumstances from God's perspective and revelation from the Word of God, we understand Jesus was scourged and beaten for the purposes of providing wholeness and healing to those who call on the Name of Jesus. To the casual, unenlightened onlooker, Jesus's suffering and death happened because He was challenging the religious leaders who had accused him of breaking their laws. To believers with insight and revelation by the Holy Spirit, Jesus's suffering and death occurred by God's plan for redemption, as this fulfilled all the prophecies recorded in the scriptures.

One of those many prophecies states the wounds on the Messiah's body brought healing to people. It was His bodily suffering that accomplished our physical healing. His blood purchased forgiveness of sins and eternal life; His body brought healing in this life. This passage in Isaiah is the prophecy speaking of this great truth.

His blood purchased forgiveness of sins and eternal life; His body brought healing in this life.

> "Surely he has borne our griefs and carried our sor-
> rows; yet we esteemed him stricken, smitten by
> God, and afflicted. But he was wounded for our
> transgressions, he was bruised for our iniquities;
> upon him was the chastisement that made us whole,
> and with his stripes we are healed" (Is. 53.4-5).

This well-known citation from Isaiah is often quoted and memorized. It carries a great truth that came true in Jesus the Messiah.
By calling on the Name of Jesus, we connect with the provision of
this prophetic truth. Unpacking the Hebrew words in this phrase
is worthwhile: "Surely he has borne our griefs and carried our sorrows." Many other English translations also use "griefs" and "sorrows" in translating this verse. The Hebrew word for "griefs" in
this passage is חֳלִי (choli). Every other time this word occurs in the
scripture it is translated as "sicknesses" or "diseases." The Hebrew
word for "sorrows" in this passage is מַכְאוֹב (makob). Similarly
every other time this word occurs in scripture it is translated as
"pains." This well-known passage is not so accurately translated to
English in some common translations.

It should more accurately read "Surely he has borne our diseases and carried our pains." Griefs and sorrows are included in
the words choli (diseases) and makob (pains), but griefs and sorrows are diseases of the soul only. These English interpretations
are not wrong, as Jesus certainly took our griefs and sorrows, but
this neglects that Jesus's body was stricken for our physical, emo-
tional, and spiritual healing and wholeness. This prophecy about
the Messiah speaks clearly of the healing of the physical body by
the stripes, the wounds, the suffering of Jesus in His body.

The gospel according to Matthew quotes this same passage
from Isaiah. The Greek words in this passage accurately characterize the meaning of these Hebrew words. The translation from
Greek to English is accurate.

That evening they brought to him many who were possessed with demons; and he cast out the spirits with a word, and healed all who were sick. This was to fulfil what was spoken by the prophet Isaiah, "He took our infirmities and bore our diseases" (Matt. 8.16-17).

The Greek words chosen in translation of the Isaiah passage are "nosos" for "choli" (infirmities) and "astheneia" for "makob" (diseases). Nosos is a Greek word for disease, sickness, a chronic persisting disease, typically incurable. We use this Greek root in medical terminology. (A nosocomial infection is an infection acquired in the hospital.) "Astheneia" is a Greek word for weakness, frailty, an inability to do because of disease. These Greek words used to translate the Isaiah prophecy are consistent representations of the original Hebrew text.[3]

So to discern the body is to recognize, understand, and honor the sufferings of Jesus's physical body for our health and wholeness. This is the first of three understandings to explain the meaning of "discerning the body." 1st

CHRIST'S BODY, THE CHURCH

A second understanding of "discerning the body" states that the body is the church. Believers who call on the Name of Jesus make up the body of Christ. Jesus is the head and believers together comprise His body. Since Jesus's ascension His body is now the church. "Christ is the head of the church, his body, and is himself its Savior."[4] The body of Christ, His church, has varieties of gifts given by Jesus through the Holy Spirit to make bodily growth and upbuild itself in love.

This understanding of discerning the body is to recognize that the regular people taking communion with you in church have gifts given by Jesus through the Holy Spirit. The person next to you may be someone you know well. You may think of him as a good athlete or of her as a teacher that your child had some years ago. You may encounter someone in the fellowship area of your church who is lawyer so you might ask a legal question because you recognize an expertise in that person. Yet this same person, a Christian lawyer, is part of the body of Christ and therefore has the workings and message of God within. You can be taken with his expertise in legal matters and miss the provision that can come from God through this person. You may rightly discern his legal prowess and miss the spiritual gifts he has as part of the body of Christ.

The members of your church are members of Christ's body. Every one of them is a sinner in need of grace, just as you are. So you may also bring to mind some things you know about that needed forgiveness, as no member of the body of Christ is without sin. You may be mindful of the humanness, the sinfulness of the one next to you taking the Lord's Supper. So with this mindset you might not expect to encounter the gifts of the Spirit coming through that same person as part of Christ's body, the church.

This very thing happened to Jesus Himself. The people in the synagogue, where Jesus read from Isaiah as recorded in Luke chapter 4, similarly disregarded His message because they held Him only in His human form. He read these words which speak of the Spirit of the Lord working through Him: "The Spirit of the Lord is upon me, because he has anointed me to preach good news to the poor. He has sent me to proclaim release to the captives and recovering of sight to the blind, to set at liberty those who are oppressed, to proclaim the acceptable year of the Lord."[5]

Then He proclaimed this word of prophecy was fulfilled before them on that day. Jesus declared before those assembled in that synagogue that He was this One sent by God. Before long someone spoke up and said, "Isn't that the carpenter, Joseph's son?" This was someone in the crowd essentially saying, "Wait, we know this man, how can He be the fulfillment of a prophecy? He grew up with us. We know His family. We're not going to let Him out of the box we have put Him in. We have a label for Him and this doesn't fit."

It took just one person in this synagogue gathering to speak out and cause the whole gathering to question Him. The Word of God says they took offense at Him. That is, they chose to keep Jesus in the role and status of life they had for Him. This was taking offense at Him. They did not discern who He was. They would not see Him as anything other than their assigned position for Him.

They took offense at Him, not discerning the body, and so they did not receive what He offered. Rather they drove Him out of the synagogue. They did not receive Him. They did not discern the body of the Messiah in their midst and thus brought judgment upon themselves.

The Messiah appeared in human form. It was an ordinary human who was the Messiah. The people did not discern, recognize, or honor Him for who He was. They saw Him as one of themselves and did not receive what God provided for them through the Messiah, who up until then was known as a carpenter, Joseph's son. Jesus came in lowly fashion without fanfare or prominent position. This Prophet was without honor in His own synagogue. They took offense at Him because He made claims related to the Isaiah prophecy while being just a carpenter, Joseph's son. They did not recognize Him as the Messiah. They did not discern the body.

The same can happen in any gathering of believers today. The gifts of Jesus given to the church are residing in regular people next to you. Someone who stands up to read the Word of God today could be known as a daughter of one of the church council members, a college student studying working toward a communications major, or viewed as a carpenter's son. Though recognizing these identities, it is possible to not discern the gifts of God which reside in that person you perhaps have known since childhood. This college student, when believing in Jesus and filled by the promised Holy Spirit, does in fact have within himself the same power that raised Jesus from the dead. This ordinary person reading a scripture in church also has been given gifts from God for edifying the church.

How often do we miss the workings of God that would come to us through regular people we know? We like to receive something directly from God, but almost always He provides through people. It is possible to ask from God and simultaneously neglect or refuse His answer or provision because it comes through ordinary people around us. Failure to recognize this is not discerning the body. *2nd*

HONOR

Conversely, each time we join in the gathering of believers we can look for these gifts and provisions from the Father through His people. When we assemble for worship and the Word, we can anticipate that Jesus will speak and act through His body, the church. Moreover, we can even draw out of these same people the gifts of the Holy Spirit within them by encouraging them to not neglect the gifts of God given them. We can call forth and release these latent gifts by words of prophecy, encouragement, and prayers of impartation.

It is possible to ask from God and simultaneously neglect or refuse His answer or provision because it comes through ordinary people around us.

Too often church-goers view one another as just neighbors, fellows in the same ship (fellowship), a vocalist in the choir, a volunteer for Sunday school, etc. without remembering these same people are members of the body of Christ who have the same power residing in them that raised Jesus from the dead. These ordinary appearing people are in fact seated with Christ in the heavenly places and have been given gifts for building up this body of Christ.

100

Encouraging and building up one another to avoid neglecting these scriptural truths about our identities is vitally important.

Such words and actions that show honor to others function to bring out the fruits and gifts of the Spirit in others. How important it is to show honor to one another. It is a deliberate choice to respect and love one another as believers and members one of another in the body of Christ. This is discerning the body and brings health and wholeness in the church.

Outdo one another in showing honor (Rom. 12.10).

Honor all men. Love the brotherhood. Fear God. Honor the emperor (1 Pet. 2.17).

YOUR BODY

A third understanding of this phrase "discern the body" can refer to an individual's own physical body. In this regard, Paul is instructing believers to examine and judge themselves, to prepare for receiving the elements of the Lord's Supper, to participate rightly in the body and blood of the Lord Jesus Christ, remembering His sacrifice for the forgiveness of sins and the healing and wholeness of our bodies, souls, and spirits.

Discern your own body to evaluate whether you are partaking in the Lord's Supper properly. Understand your body was crucified with Christ. "For you have died, and your life is hid with Christ in God."[6] The life you now live in the flesh (in your body), you live by faith in the Son of God. Recognize the Name of Jesus is invoked over you, is upon you, and you are named by Him.

To discern your body is also to recognize the same Spirit that raised Jesus from the dead now dwells in you, the believer. It is to understand that this same Spirit is working His gifts and calling in you to benefit others in the church and advance His kingdom in the world. You are not alone when you believe in Jesus. When you invite Jesus into your heart, He brings all His friends with Him. You are a member of His body along with all the other members.

The Name of Jesus is upon every believer as we established earlier. So being in Christ and under His Name, now as His body, the church, is itself the discernment of the body that we must understand to prevent weakness, illness, and death. We must recognize the Name of Jesus and the gifts He gave to His body, the church, from His physical body.

Paul combines all three of these understandings of discerning the body when he writes to the Colossians about his own role as a minister. He speaks of Christ's physical body, the church as His body, and his own physical body in this one verse in Col. 1.24: "Now I rejoice in my sufferings for your sake, and in my flesh I complete what is lacking in Christ's afflictions for the sake of his body, the church."

Chapter 10

ABOVE EVERY OTHER NAME

There are well-known names of powerful people who lived throughout history including leaders such as Julius Caesar, Napoleon Bonaparte, Hitler, Alexander the Great, Joan of Arc, Winston Churchill, etc. Current world political leaders are names also widely recognized throughout most of the world as they are in positions of great power. There are other names of people who are well-known because of inventions or discoveries. Among them are Isaac Newton, Albert Einstein, Thomas Edison, Nikola Tesla, etc. The names of these people are widely recognized.

Other names, not referring to people, are also related to great power. The sun's gravity is powerful. Tornadoes, earthquakes, tsunamis are great forces of nature. Names of principalities and powers in the unseen world of angels and demons also have a degree of power. And there are other types of names that describe certain diseases which are incurable and/or cause great suffering. All of these have names that conjure images and feelings in most people.

MORE POWERFUL

The Name of Jesus is above all of these names. The Name of Jesus is greater, more powerful, more wonderful, more amazing, more beautiful. His Name is above every other name. The qualities represented in His Name are above any quality referenced in any other name.

There is great power in the Name of Jesus. Jesus Himself is all-powerful. His Name is also all-powerful. There is power in the Name. Every knee, in heaven and on earth and under the earth, will bow at this Name. Every tongue will confess Jesus is Lord. No other Name is greater than the Name of Jesus. Every other name is subject to the Name of Jesus because God has set His Name above every name.

So Jesus's Name is authoritative over any other name. His Name is greater than any President, King, or governmental authority. His Name is authoritative over cancer, arthritis, and every other name for sickness, infirmity, and disease. His Name is exalted far above any noun referencing any and all persons, places, and things.

When Jesus spoke to the wind and storm, to the sycamine tree, to the ones needing forgiveness and healing, there was power that went forth. When believers effectively use the Name of Jesus, the same power that raised Jesus from the dead is employed. A word of command spoken in Jesus's Name invokes a greater Name over any other object, disease, situation, spirit, or person. When the Name of Jesus is spoken over the name of any disease or infirmity, any spirit or demon, any mountain, the Name of Jesus stands as victor as His Name is above all these Names. Jesus's Name is given to the church. This Name is given to be used by believers to bring glory to the Father.

> *When believers effectively use the Name of Jesus, the same power that raised Jesus from the dead is employed.*

We can use His Name. When we invoke the Name of Jesus as ones who abide in Him and in the Father, we are calling upon a greater force, a superior position, a Name above every other name given to the church to use in prayer, thanksgiving, word of command, and deeds of obedience. The Name of Jesus is authoritative over every other name.

ON THAT DAY

God's Son was with Him before creation. From the beginning He is called "The Word of God." He was with God at the time of creation and functioned as the agent of creation.[1] Then, in the fullness of time, God proclaimed the Name of His Son to Mary and Joseph. They were told to name Him "Jesus" or "Jeshua", which means "Messiah", the One who will save us from our sins. He received this Name at His birth, but it was at His resurrection that God made Him to sit at His right hand. On that day, when He was resurrected from the dead, His Name, the Name Jesus, was then set above every other name in heaven and earth, in this age and the age to come.

God has put all things under His feet and has made Him head over all things for the church.[2] The Word of God who was with God in the beginning, being one with God, came to earth as a baby born of Mary and the Holy Spirit. He was then given the Name Jesus. Later, at His resurrection, God made this same Word of God, His Son named Jesus, who preexisted creation, to sit at His right hand and declared ON THAT DAY that His Name, the Name of Jesus, is the Name which is above every other name for all time and places, even beyond time and creation.

Look closely at Phil. 2.8-11. THAT DAY was at Jesus's death and resurrection when His Name was exalted high above every other name. Jesus was with God from the beginning as the Word of God. He was named Jesus at His birth just as every other human acquires a name. However, it was at His death and resurrection that God made the Name of Jesus to be above every other name.

And being found in human form he humbled himself and became obedient unto death, even death on a cross. Therefore God has highly exalted him and bestowed on him the name which is above every name, that at the name of Jesus every knee should bow, in heaven and on earth and under the earth, and every tongue confess that Jesus Christ is Lord, to the glory of God the Father (Phil. 2.8-11).

The person of Jesus was pre-existent with the Father before creation. The Name "Jesus" was given to Him, as the Word of God now in human form, when He was born of Mary. The exalted Name of Jesus occurred at His death and resurrection. The superiority of Jesus's Name over every other name was established by God, not when He was born of Mary, but when He was raised from the dead. On that day God made His Name above every other name. See what the writer of Hebrews says about the acquired name given to the Word of God, the Son of God.

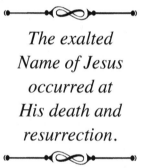

The exalted Name of Jesus occurred at His death and resurrection.

He reflects the glory of God and bears the very stamp of his nature, upholding the universe by his word of power. When he had made purification for sins, he sat down at the right hand of the Majesty on high, having become as much superior to angels as the name he has obtained is more excellent than theirs. For to what angel did God ever say, "Thou are my Son, today I have begotten thee"? Or again, "I will be to him a father, and he shall be to me a son"? (Heb. 1.3-5).

The Son of God is eternal. His Names are eternal. He existed before creation as the Word of God.[3] At His birth He is named Jesus. At His death and resurrection, His Name is exalted above every other name. Back in heaven after His ascension, His Name is called the Word of God.

> He is clad in a robe dipped in blood, and the name by which he is called is The Word of God (Rev. 19.13).

So here are the Names for the Son of God through the span of time:

- At creation (and before creation): The Word of God (John 1.1-3, 14).
- At His birth: Jesus, Emmanuel (Luke 1.31, Matt. 1.25).
- At His resurrection: Jesus, above every other name (Phil. 2.8-11).
- Back in heaven with the Father: The Word of God (Rev. 19.13).

Why did God cause Jesus's Name to be exalted at His resurrection? Why, when the Word of God existed with God as God before creation, would Jesus' Name be placed above every name at the time of His resurrection?

This is so for two primary reasons: 1) He humbled himself to become human flesh. He who ascended to the heavens had to descend first from heaven. When He descended he acquired the Name Jesus, which is Emmanuel, God with us. When he ascended His given Name at birth was then exalted above every name.[4] 2) His exalted Name is now given to the church. At the time of His resurrection, the church came into being as the body of Jesus Christ. As His body, the church bears the Name of the Head of the body.

The bride takes the Name of the Bridegroom. His exalted Name is given to the church, with all the power, glory, majesty, wonder and awe, access to the Father, salvation, provision, deliverance, healing.

This exalted Name is The Name given to the church. God made Him head over all things FOR THE CHURCH.[5] It was better for Jesus to return this way to His Father as His Name is now given to the church to carry on the work of the ministry, to depict the church's oneness with Jesus as the bride of Christ, to inherit the kingdom of God, to pray to the Father just as Jesus did. This Name is now given to the church.

This exalted Name is The Name given to the church.

Blessed be thy glorious name which is exalted above all blessing and praise" (Neh. 9.5).

O Lord, our Lord, how majestic is thy name in all the earth! Thou whose glory above the heavens is chanted (Ps. 8.1).

I bow down toward thy holy temple and give thanks to thy name for thy steadfast love and thy faithfulness; for thou hast exalted above everything thy name and thy word (Ps. 138.2).

Let them praise the name of the Lord, for his name alone is exalted; his glory is above earth and heaven (Ps. 148.13).

Chapter 11

IN JESUS'S NAME

The Word of God recorded in the Old and New Testaments contains extra emphasis on the Name. Here are some examples. Zeph. 3.12 states, "They shall seek refuge in the name of the Lord." This verse says refuge is sought and found in His Name. The Lord Himself is a refuge, but the Name of the Lord is where refuge is found.

Solomon wrote about his father David's desire: "Now it was in the heart of David my father to build a house for the name of the Lord, the God of Israel."[1] The building of the temple was for the Name.

As another example, "Everyone who calls upon the Name of the Lord will be saved."[2] Here again it is the Lord who saves us. Everyone who calls upon Him will be saved. But the focus is on the Name. Everyone who calls upon the NAME of the Lord will be saved. There is no other Name by which we can be saved.[3] The eternal destiny for each human is vested in a Name.

There are many such examples throughout scripture where the Name of the Lord is referenced. Why does scripture refer so frequently to the NAME of the Lord? We are to call upon the Name

> *The eternal destiny for each human is vested in a Name.*

of the Lord. We can call upon the Lord, but we are to call upon His Name. We can praise and bless the Lord, but we are instructed to praise and bless the Name of the Lord. Why is this expressed and accented in scripture? What is it about His Name?

Phrases such as "the Name of the Lord," "My Name," "Thy Name," "Name sake," "Jesus's Name," and "the Father's Name" occur well over 400 times in the Bible. The prepositional phrases "in Jesus's Name," "in My Name," and "in Him" occur throughout the New Testament. The frequency of these phrases in the Word of God demand our focus, attention, and understanding. This is so because The Name is given to believers, because the Name validates and releases God's promises, because the Name itself brings salvation, healing, empowering, protection, and all the blessings and provisions promised in the Word of God.

IN THE NAME OF ...

What is the meaning of the phrase "in the name of..."? We use this prepositional phrase in several ways in our day by day communications.

"In the name of..." can mean "by the authority of..." For example, "Stop, in the name of the law." Here the name makes reference to the law as an authority that strengthens the command to stop. The power of the law is invoked by saying the phrase "in the name of the law."

"In the name of..." can also be used to speak on behalf of someone else. It can mean "on behalf of ..." For example, "She made a donation in her son's name." Here the donation is made by this woman and done so on behalf of her son, as though it were coming directly from him or in memory of her son.

An additional use of the phrase "in the name of..." is to make an appeal. For example, "What, in the name of decency, are you doing?" This usage calls forth a certain quality or character as a reference or standard.

"In the name of ..." can mean "under the designation of..." or "for purposes of..." Here is an example: "They burned idols in the name of piety." This usage justifies a certain action based on established beliefs or convictions.

Furthermore, "in the name of..." can hearken to possession and ownership of something or someone. The legal right of power of attorney is authorization to act on behalf of someone else, to use the name of that person for legal purposes including management and distribution of funds, possessions, and other decisions pertaining to another's personal and financial affairs.

The biblical usage of the phrase "in the Name of Jesus" communicates all of these meanings. The Name of Jesus, which is given to the church, carries the authority of His being, His message and ministry, the benefits of His atoning work on the cross, and the immeasurable power that raised Him from the dead. "In the Name of Jesus" associates all of these truths.

FOR MY NAME'S SAKE

The Spirit of God in a revelation to John at the island of Patmos said to the church at Ephesus, "I know you are enduring patiently and bearing up for **my name's sake**, and you have not grown weary (emphasis mine)."[4]

The phrases "for My Name's sake," "for the sake of My Name," "Jesus's sake", "His sake," or "the Lord's sake" occur 19 times in the New Testament. Nine of these make reference specifically to His Name. Six of these nine verses are statements regarding how disciples of Jesus will suffer and be hated for His Name's sake (see Matt. 10.22, 24.9; Mark 13.13; Luke 21.12, 21.17; Acts 9.16). The other three verses pertain to the message and ministry of His disciples:

- And every one who has left houses and brothers or sisters or father or mother or children or lands, for my name's sake, will receive a hundredfold, and inherit eternal life (Matt. 19.29).

- …through whom we have received grace and apostleship to bring about the obedience of faith for the sake of his name among the nations (Rom. 1.5).
- I know you are enduring patiently and bearing up for my name's sake, and you have not grown weary (Rev. 2.3).

"My Name's sake" refers to Jesus's cause, His purpose, His motives, reasons, interests, and concerns. So the statements of Jesus about how His followers will be hated for His Name's sake refer to being aligned with Jesus's stuff – His words, actions, His being. It is a reference to all the things about Jesus as recorded in the Word of God. Furthermore, His Name's sake is a specific reference to His Name. These scriptures state, "My Name's sake," not "Jesus's sake." Because of the Name of Jesus, these things are so. Again these scriptures could state these truths about Jesus Himself, but the focus is on His Name. This focus on the Name is throughout the Old and New Testaments.

> He leads me in paths of righteousness for his name's sake (Ps. 23.3).

THE EARLY CHURCH

Jesus's Name had meaning in the early church. The apostles and disciples went forth to preach, teach, heal, and deliver. All of this was done in the Name of Jesus. The early church believers understood their unity with Christ and identified with His message, His death, and His resurrection. Therefore it was with great power and with great results that their ministry flourished.

They also encountered great resistance because of Jesus's Name. So His Name was also recognized outside of His followers.

Those who opposed Jesus and His followers recognized the power of His Name. The believers of the early church were forbidden to teach in Jesus's Name. "We strictly charged you not to teach in this name, yet here you have filled Jerusalem with your teaching and you intend to bring this man's blood upon us."[5] They were not simply teaching some philosophies and human wisdom. They were teaching in His Name. This made all the difference.

Paul wrote to the Corinthians saying he decided to know nothing among them except Jesus Christ and Him crucified. With this focus in his message to the Corinthians there was demonstration of the Spirit and the power of the Name of Jesus.[6]

IDENTIFICATION

The prepositional phrase "in Him" is woven throughout the New Testament. This simple phrase has great meaning, pointing to the intimate relationship between a believer and the Savior. "In Him" describes both the identification Christ has made with those who believe in Him and the identification a believer makes with Christ. We are in Him and He is in us. To be "in Him" is to abide in Him and He in us.[7]

This is not just believing in certain tenets; it is experiential.

The believer's identification with Christ involves accepting and believing His message and accomplished work. This is not just believing in certain tenets; it is experiential. The believer is actually crucified with Christ and then raised up with Him into newness of life.

The Apostle Paul stated this identification with Jesus's death and resurrection. He describes the same for all those who are baptized into His Name, being united with Him in His death and resurrection.

> I have been crucified with Christ; it is no longer I
> who live, but Christ who lives in me; and the life
> I now live in the flesh I live by faith in the Son
> of God, who loved me and gave himself for me
> (Gal. 2.20).

> Do you not know that all of us who have been bap-
> tized into Christ Jesus were baptized into his death?
> We were buried therefore with him by baptism into
> death, so that as Christ was raised from the dead by
> the glory of the Father, we too might walk in new-
> ness of life. For if we have been united with him in a
> death like his, we shall certainly be united with him
> in a resurrection like his. We know that our old self
> was crucified with him so that the sinful body might
> be destroyed, and we might no longer be enslaved
> to sin. For he who has died is freed from sin. But if
> we have died with Christ, we believe that we shall
> also live with him (Rom. 6.3-8).

To be "in Him" is to identify with His Name. Those who are "in Christ" are thereby authorized and empowered to use the Name of Jesus in prayer, thanksgiving, teaching, and ministry.

BELIEVE THE NAME

Scripture states we are to believe in God, in Jesus His Son, and in the Holy Spirit. Additionally, we are to believe in the Name. Here again is the concentrated attention on the Name.

> And this is his commandment, that we should
> *believe in the name* of his Son Jesus Christ and love
> one another, just as he has commanded us (1 John
> 3.23, emphasis mine).

114

> I write this to you who *believe in the name* of the
> Son of God, that you may know that you have
> eternal life (1 John 5.13, emphasis mine).

The Name of Jesus is power. His Name embodies who He is and what He has done. But the Name itself is wonderful, beautiful, exalted, and powerful. Let's carefully and boldly use the Name in ways consistent with the One who bears the Name.

SECTION FOUR

USE THE NAME

We have considered the purposes and functions of any name. We have explored the Names for God and the exalted Name of Jesus Christ. This last section attends to strategies for a believer to use the Name of Jesus. Consideration is given to proper attitudes and usage of His Name as instructed in the Word of God.

Chapter 12

STRATEGIES FOR USE

MOSES'S STAFF

The Name of Jesus, when properly used by the church, is like the rod ("staff" in some translations) that God gave to Moses. This rod was used by Moses as a display of God's power. Moses is the only person in recorded history to use a rod as a gift from God to release His power. Through this tool he saw great miracles of God occur as he obeyed God's orders. When he threw the rod down, it became a snake. When he picked it up it became a staff again. The Lord said, "You shall take in your hand this rod, with which you shall do the signs."[1] When Moses struck the river Nile with the rod it turned to blood. As Moses stretched forth the rod as the Lord instructed, there were frogs, gnats, thunder, hail, and locusts. When Moses lifted up the rod and stretched his hand over the sea as he was told to do, the strong winds blew to divide the sea and allow the Hebrews to cross on dry ground. After crossing the sea he stretched his hand over the sea behind them and the waters rushed in on the Pharoah and the Egyptians pursuing them.

We are not given a rod such as Moses used. We are given the Name of Jesus. How do we use the Name of Jesus effectively? Let's consider how did this rod work for Moses? First, Moses was careful to do everything the Lord had told him. He was therefore abiding in Father God. God saw Moses's obedient heart and actions as worthy of possessing and using God's power. Secondly, the rod in Moses's hand was empowered by God. It was a regular rod, rather ordinary, unspecial. It was an earthly object set apart for God to perform signs and wonders. Moses could not accomplish his heavenly mission with earthly tools alone. Thirdly, the rod was Moses's to use. When the rod was employed, God's power was released. It was required of Moses to use the rod. Nothing would happen if he did not use the rod God gave him. When he did use it as the Lord instructed, mighty events occurred.

When God parted the Red Sea for the Hebrew people to cross, He had Moses lift up the rod and stretch out his hand over the water. God could have parted the sea without Moses's use of the rod, but He did not. God performed this miracle as Moses obeyed God. Here we see some of God's nature: He does His mighty works through His people who obey Him. When Moses stretched forth the rod, the hand of God was moved to release His power for demonstrations of His power. Had Moses not lifted up the rod and stretched out his hand over the water, the seas would not have parted, even though it was God's will. God has all power to do whatever He wishes, but He usually accomplishes His purposes through His people who obey Him.

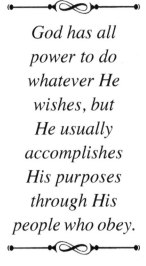

God has all power to do whatever He wishes, but He usually accomplishes His purposes through His people who obey.

The Name of Jesus, as the rod of God, carries the authority and power of God. This Name is given to His people today to be used for the advancing of God's Kingdom. God uses Jesus's body, the church, to advance His Kingdom. He has given us the rod of God, the Name of Jesus, to carry out this task. God could bypass the church and display His power sovereignly, without working through people, but He generally does not do this. Rather He has given His Son's Name to the church for us to use in obedience to God's will.

The Egyptians could have stolen that rod from Moses, but what they could not take was the Name given to the church. It can be spoken by believers to engage the power of God. Though the Name cannot be stolen like a thief might steal property, the Name can be invoked and yet appear ineffective. Using the Name to attempt to endorse selfish ambitions and prayers will not wield its great power.

The Name of Jesus remains great and above every name, but its improper use can make that great Name appear less than great. When there is disbelief and ignorance in the church regarding the power and authority of Jesus's Name, when its proper use is distorted without an understanding of the will and purpose of that Name, and when believers are neglecting to abide in the Father and His Son, this great Name is not functioning effectively in the church. Repeated misunderstanding and misuse eventually becomes a poor witness in the church and in the world, even bringing seasoned believers to concoct certain theologies to explain this.

Most churches today have lost the power in the Name of Jesus and are reduced to a shorn Sampson. How we have fallen from our high position. One can go into the average church and hear men and women pleading with God for Him to do what He told us to do with the spiritual gifts He gives to members of His body, the church. One can hear bemoaning of weakness and inability to meet the crisis of the time. If they only knew the truth of the Name of Jesus, they would seek God's Word and will and use His Name.

Sometimes when the Name of Jesus is invoked, it occurs at the end of a prayer offered up to God requesting some worldly desires to fulfil certain passions outside of the will and word of that great Name. The power of the Name of Jesus occurs when His Name is invoked for His will and purposes, not as an attempt to endorse a carnal request. When a believer's will is to do His will, delighting

121

in the Lord, his desires become united with God's desires, thereby wielding the power of the Name of Jesus.

DAVID AND GOLIATH

The army of Israel was facing Goliath and the Philistine army. No one of them would come before their champion. His size and physical strength, along with his weapons and shielding, struck fear in the Hebrew army. They were paralyzed as they compared Goliath and his weapons with their most valiant warriors. Goliath stood about nine-to-ten feet tall and wore heavy armor. The head of his spear weighed about 25 lbs. Saul's soldiers were viewing this battle from the perspective of their own resources. These two armies were encamped opposite one another for 40 days while Goliath repeatedly called for anyone to fight him, but no one would take him on in battle.

During this time David was assigned by his father to bring food to his older brothers who were enlisted in Saul's army. David heard Goliath's defying rants and saw how the men fled from him and were much afraid. So David went to Saul saying he would go fight the Philistine giant. Saul looked at David with the same perspective as did his brothers and others in his army. Saul looked upon his outward appearance and saw he was young and not experienced in warfare. David stated he had killed lions and bears that came after his sheep. He knew it was the Lord who had delivered him from lions and bears and would also deliver him from Goliath.

Saul approved (maybe because no one else would go fight), allowing David to take on the Philistine giant. He said to him, "Go, and the LORD be with you!" How often is this saying uttered without any expectation that God's greatness and power will in fact act. Having said "the Lord be with you," Saul reverted back immediately to the worldly weapons of warfare. He loaded David down with armor he was not accustomed to. David tried these on but soon put them off as it burdened him down. He approached

Goliath with his staff and five smooth pebbles for his sling. But David had much more. He had the Name of the Lord and went in the Name of the Lord.

David used the Name when he approached Goliath. He knew about the Name of the Lord. He knew the Lord delivered him from the lions and bears. He knew the Lord God was the One fighting this battle. He spoke boldly from his knowledge of the Lord, so he was able to use the Name because of his relationship with the Lord.

> Then David said to the Philistine, "You come to me with a sword and with a spear and with a javelin; but **I come to you in the name of the LORD of hosts**, the God of the armies of Israel, whom you have defied. This day the LORD will deliver you into my hand, and I will strike you down, and cut off your head; and I will give the dead bodies of the host of the Philistines this day to the birds of the air and to the wild beasts of the earth; that all the earth may know that there is a God in Israel, and that all this assembly may know that the LORD saves not with sword and spear; for the battle is the LORDS and he will give you into our hand" (1 Sam. 17.45-47).

David states his purpose for taking on Goliath in the Name of the Lord. He is careful to designate three truths as he spoke his purpose to Goliath: 1) that all the earth may know that there is a God in Israel; 2) that all this assembly may know the LORD saves not with sword and spear; 3) that the battle is the Lord's. None of these statements came from David's own agenda. He came against Goliath in the Name of the Lord, not in his own name, not with his own agenda, not with any selfish ambition. This was a right and proper use of the Name of the Lord to defeat Goliath.

The church today is juxtaposed against the kingdom of darkness and is often either neglecting the battle, losing the battle, or attempting to engage warfare with worldly weapons. Like Saul and his army, the church lacks David-like awareness of the great Name of the Lord. The weapons of our warfare are divinely powerful for breaking down strongholds.[2]

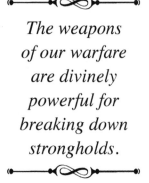

The weapons of our warfare are divinely powerful for breaking down strongholds.

PAUL'S STRATEGY

When Paul came to the Corinthians, he intentionally did not preach in lofty words or wisdom, rather he testified to and demonstrated God's power, so their faith would not rest in the wisdom of men, but in the power of God.

> When I came to you, brethren, I did not come proclaiming the testimony of God in lofty words of wisdom. For I decided to know nothing among you except Jesus Christ and him crucified. And I was with you in weakness and much trembling; and my speech and my message were not in plausible words of wisdom, but in demonstration of the Spirit and of power, that your faith might not rest in the wisdom of men but in the power of God (1 Cor. 2.1-5).

Paul had just come from Athens, as recorded in Acts 17, where he was evangelizing by using persuasion and philosophical arguments. Athens was the place where there was a statue in the center of the city with the inscription "To an unknown God." Paul used this well-known phrase to generate discussion with others, hoping to persuade them to believe in Jesus, the One who makes the Father God known. This brought about meager results as just a few people joined the Christian faith and a few others said they would like to hear more.

Then Paul left Athens and went to Corinth.[3] So when he writes in verse 1 of 1 Corinthians 2, "When I came to you...", we can see a shift in Paul's evangelism strategy as he left behind the scant results in Athens. When he came to the Corinthians, he did not come with words of wisdom, but with demonstration of the Spirit and of power. The Corinthian church was established on this strategy of power evangelism in the Name of Jesus. Paul wanted believers' faith to rest in the power of God, not in some lofty words of wisdom. The power of God is expressed and released in the great Name of Jesus.

Later in the 4th chapter, Paul states, "For the kingdom of God does not consist in talk, but in power."[4] Some of the people Paul was addressing were arrogant. They were essentially "educated" with an attitude. Paul planned to come to find out not about the talk of these arrogant people, but their power. The truth, as taught in the Name of Jesus, is not just informative; it is powerful for salvation,

Church doctrine is not so holy if it is lacking the power of the Name of Jesus and the Kingdom of God.

for changing lives, for healing, for restoration. Church doctrine is not so holy if it is lacking the power of the Name of Jesus and the Kingdom of God.

Chapter 13

SEVENFOLD RIGHT TO USE THE NAME

We discussed in chapter 1 the first name that was spoken occurred before creation. Then in chapter 5 we looked at when God revealed His Name to Moses as "I AM THAT I AM." We see in chapter 10 that God instructed Mary to name their Son "Jesus" and how God, at Jesus's death and resurrection, made His Name to be above every other name. Now let's look at how this great Name is given to us. Let's understand our right and commission to use the Name of Jesus. The authority and commission to use the Name of Jesus is sevenfold, with seven truths in the Word of God that establish our position, calling, and commission.

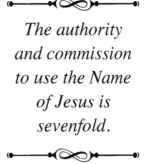

The authority and commission to use the Name of Jesus is sevenfold.

BORN INTO THE FAMILY

Most human beings are born into a family with a family name. This surname is established by God (Eph. 3.14-15: "For this reason I bow my knees before the Father, from whom every family in heaven and on earth is named.") Every human is born of a mother and father and at birth, by default, acquires a surname.

When a person becomes a Christian, hearing the Word of truth and believing in Jesus, he is born into the family of God.[1] Being born into God's family brings an inheritance which includes the Name. Just as a newborn child acquires the family name, so a newborn Christian acquires the Name. Just as a woman takes her husband's family name at marriage, so the believer takes the Name of Jesus as her bridegroom.

BAPTIZED INTO THE NAME

We are baptized into the Name, and being baptized in the Name, we are baptized into Christ Himself. In baptism we are united with Christ in His death and resurrection.

> Do you not know that all of us who have been baptized into Christ Jesus were baptized into his death? We were buried therefore with him by baptism into death, so that as Christ was raised from the dead by the glory of the Father, we too might walk in newness of life. For if we have been united with him in a death like his, we shall certainly be united with him in a resurrection like his (Rom. 6.3-5).

Believers are baptized into the Name of the Father, the Son, and the Holy Spirit. So in baptism we are united with Him and so we bear His Name.

INVOKED OVER YOU

Typically we are the ones who invoke or entreat, petition, or call upon the presence of the Lord. In more traditional churches this happens at what is called the invocation. This is a statement that the gathering of the people occurs in the Name of the Father, and of the Son, and of the Holy Spirit.

The second chapter of James depicts the opposite, where Jesus's Name is invoked over us. It occurs in the context of the partiality that the rich might show toward the poor. James 2.7 says "Is it not they who blaspheme that honorable name which was invoked over you?" This scripture says the Name of Jesus is invoked over you. That is to say, His Name is applied on you, covered over you. Jesus brought you to His Father who now sees His beloved Son when He looks upon you. His honorable Name is invoked over each believer to impute righteousness, cover with protection, and authorize the use of that Name.

PUT UPON YOU

The well-known blessing recorded in Numbers chapter 6 is spoken for purposes of putting the Lord's Name upon His people. God instructed Moses to say to Aaron and his sons how to bless the people of Israel.

> The Lord bless you and keep you; The Lord make his face to shine upon you, and be gracious to you; the Lord lift up his countenance upon you, and give you peace. So shall they put my name upon the people of Israel, and I will bless them (Num. 6.24-27).

God's intent for these spoken words of blessing was to put His Name upon them. When the Lord's Name is put upon you by way of blessings, you are authorized to bear that Name and use that Name.

CALLED BY HIS NAME

Another well-known scripture comes from 2 Chron. 7.14: "If my people who are called by my name humble themselves, and pray and seek my face, and turn from their wicked ways, then I will hear from heaven, and will forgive their sin and heal their land." This word from God shows He calls His people by His Name. "If my people who are called by my name…" God is speaking to certain people, those who are His people, ones who have been called, called by His Name. Deut. 28.10 states the same truth: "And all the people of the earth shall see that you are called by the name of the Lord." Those called by His Name are empowered to offer repentant, effectual prayer so that He hears, forgives, and heals.

POWER OF ATTORNEY

A person who has been given power of attorney is able to sign documents in behalf of someone else with the same authority as if these documents were signed originally. When my father was 95 years old he assigned me as one with power of attorney. I was then able to write checks and sign other documents for him as if it were he that did so. The believer's use of the Name of Jesus is a power of attorney. We are to go in His Name, thank in His Name, ask in His Name, heal in His Name, bless in His Name, do everything in His Name.

COMMISSIONED TO GO, MAKE DISCIPLES, AND TEACH

The great commission recorded in Matthew 28 gives believers the assignment to go and herald this Name among the nations. "And Jesus came and said to them, "All authority in heaven and on earth has been given to me. Go therefore and make disciples of all nations, baptizing them in the name of the Father and of the Son and of the Holy Spirit, teaching them to observe all that I have commanded you."[2] We are commissioned as ambassadors carrying His Name.

If you are a child of God, then you are an heir of God, a joint heir with Christ.

If you are a child of God, then you are an heir of God, a joint heir with Christ. You have a right to use the Name of Jesus because of your place in the family, because you are baptized into His Name, because His Name is invoked over you and put upon you, because you are called by His Name, because you are given the power of attorney in using His Name, and because you are commissioned by that Name to go, preach, teach, heal, and bless.

Chapter 14

GIVE THANKS

"He also who eats, eats in honor of the Lord, since he gives thanks to God" (Rom. 14.6).

BAKED FISH

Just after the iron curtain came down in the early 90s, I was able to make four mission trips to Russia. The last of these was with John, a leader and good friend from my home church. I had been studying Russian and was able to make small conversation without an interpreter. John knew very little Russian, but would often enter into a conversation, then look to me to translate to Russian.

The Russian Christians are beautiful people, especially the old-timers who lived through persecution for their faith. We were in the city of Volgodansk and had been invited to dinner at a home where a woman and her son resided. We learned she was a child at the time when communism was first established in Russia. She was a daughter of a Pastor who held to his faith and did not compromise his beliefs before the communist state. She recounted that during her childhood she did not live in any one place for more than three months. Often, upon hearing of officials searching for them in the area, she and her family had to gather their few belongings and move elsewhere, usually during the night. She remembers fleeing a home through the rear window as there were KGB police at the front door.

We heard about her story from her son and a few others while she was preparing the food. John began to discuss some political matters about philosophies of government. He would speak for several minutes then look to me to translate. I struggled to capture the gist of his words. My translations were much shorter than his statements.

During this time we were asked if we would like fish for dinner. I knew John did not care for fish, so I answered for both of us. John was a "no" and I was a "yes." The discussion continued in Russian, demanding all my attention to attempt to interpret, until the food was served to each of us by setting a plate before us already populated with food.

I looked down at my plate and saw a variety including salad, potatoes, beets, and fish. All of these foods were soaking in some black liquid filling the bottom of the plate. I looked at John's plate. He did not have any of the black colored liquid. I then looked at the platter where the fish was baked. I saw the head and tail of the fish. Sections of the middle were cut and served to those wanting fish. I saw the same black liquid and soon realized that the fish was baked whole, including the entrails. The guts of the fish, which were now mostly black liquid, were also baked and served. The entrails were now soaking into all the other selections of food on my plate. John looked at me with a smile as he saw what I had before me. This woman and her son, who had just one tooth with which to eat, were so honored to have us as guests to their home. I gave thanks for this food in the Name of Jesus. I ate it all, but it was not the most savory meal I have eaten.

IN ALL CIRCUMSTANCES

> "Rejoice always, pray constantly, give thanks in all
> circumstances; for this is the will of God in Christ
> Jesus for you" (1 Thess. 5.16-18).

Thanksgiving is one of two of the most powerful things we can say and do. The other one is forgiveness. Both thanksgiving and forgiveness can be offered at any time in any circumstances. They not only can be expressed, they should be. Anyone, at any time and any circumstances, can utter these two powerful expressions. When one wields the words of thanksgiving and forgiveness, the tides of eternity and the heart of God Almighty are moved. (See a discussion about the authority to forgive in my book "This Mountain").

When one wields the words of thanksgiving and forgiveness, the tides of eternity and the heart of God Almighty are moved.

Thanksgiving is a choice not dependent on our circumstances, feelings, attitudes, or beliefs. We **can** always express thanks to God and to others. We **should** always express thanks. We do not need to wait for something that makes us feel thankful. Thanksgiving is a choice, something we can say and do at any time and in any circumstance. We can and should say words of thanks that come out of our will. Such words may need to bypass our feelings, thoughts, and beliefs. The Word of God gives the imperative to thank the Father in the Name of Jesus, with no qualifiers to this command and no exceptions. "In all circumstances" includes every matter, every person, and every situation, at all times. There are no circumstances where it is not the will of God to give thanks.

Jonah gave thanks when he was in the belly of the fish. God had called him to preach repentance to Nineveh. Jonah did not want to go there because he had an attitude toward that city. He knew if they did repent God would have mercy on them and forgive them. They would not come under judgment if they repented. Jonah saw the wickedness of Nineveh and the judgment they deserved. He did not want to bring a message of repentance to them as he wanted them to come under God's judgment rather than His mercy. So he disobeyed God's command and fled to Joppa to take a boat to Tarshish.

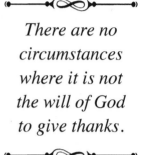

There are no circumstances where it is not the will of God to give thanks.

When a storm came up and the boat was sinking, Jonah had the crew throw him overboard. He was swallowed up by a great fish wherein he spent three days and three nights. Jonah knew he had disobeyed God's Word to him. He knew he was in his predicament because of his own actions. He knew God had put him into the waters and the belly of the fish. What did Jonah do in these circumstances? He prayed to God and gave thanks to Him. "'But I *with the voice of thanksgiving* will sacrifice to thee; what I have vowed I will pay. Deliverance belongs to the Lord!' And the Lord spoke to the fish, and it vomited out Jonah upon the dry land"[1] (italics mine). In Jonah's dire circumstances he gave thanks to God and renewed his vows. At this the Lord caused the fish to spew him out onto dry land. Give thanks in all circumstances.

Jesus demonstrated this truth at the time when he was facing His death and carrying the weight of the sins of the world. Jesus, who was about to be crucified and lose everything, knew the Father had given all things into His hands.[2] Jesus, on the night he was betrayed, gave thanks. When He was betrayed He gave thanks.

He did this to focus His mind properly. Thanksgiving to His Father came out of His abiding relationship with Him. He was able to go through the most horrible suffering and do so because of the joy was set before Him. So He gave thanks on the night He was betrayed. Jesus gave thanks at the time of His betrayal, knowing that He would suffer greatly, both physically and spiritually as He carried the trillions of sins of the world. The weight of just one sin on us is heavy. Jesus gave thanks as He looked toward the suffering of His atoning work for all the sins of humans for all time. Thanksgiving kept His heart aright so it was with joy that He endured the cross. Jesus's thanksgiving of the Father kept His mind on the right things. At His greatest time of suffering and loss He was thankful and knew He had all things given Him by His Father.

Thanksgiving cleanses the mind. A habit of thanksgiving causes the mind to be set on the things of the Spirit, bringing life and peace.[3] Giving thanks in all circumstances is powerful to fend off anxiety and fear. Such words of gratitude serve to recognize and honor the goodness of God. So give thanks IN ALL CIRCUMSTANCES as this is the will of God for you. Experience the great power of thanksgiving to take control of your mind and overrule thoughts of anxiety, fear, doubt, etc.

> *A habit of thanksgiving causes the mind to be set on the things of the Spirit, bringing life and peace.*

ALWAYS AND FOR EVERYTHING

Yet another instruction about thanksgiving is found in Paul's Epistle to the Ephesians. This goes beyond giving thanks in all circumstances. The scripture states in Eph. 5.20: "…always and for everything giving thanks in the name of our Lord Jesus Christ to God the Father."

This is giving thanks not just in the midst of all things, but giving thanks FOR EVERYTHING. We are instructed here to give thanks for everything. Everything good and bad, right and wrong, blessings and sins, happy and sad, whether bringing benefit or loss, is what we give thanks FOR.

When I have preached on this scripture verse, invariably at least one will come to me with questions: "Are you saying that I should give thanks to God for the death of my spouse?"; Are you telling me to thank God for the loss of my job?"; "Am I supposed to give thanks for my disease or infirmity?"; Are you saying God is responsible for these bad things?"; "I am not going to thank God for something He did not do."

I give thanks to God for everything as the Word of God instructs. Why? The simple, powerful answer is because we are told to do this. I do not need to understand why in order to obey. I do not need to feel it or like it to give thanks to God for everything. However, there are good reasons to give thanks FOR everything. We are to give thanks for everything as an act of the will in obedience to the Word of God, but there is also understanding and insight as to why this is appropriate.

FIRST GRADE

My oldest daughter was enrolled in first grade in our church's private Christian school. Things were going smoothly for several months until she came home saying she did not want to go to school anymore. When asked why, she said some girls were mean. Within a few weeks her sentiments escalated. She was crying when coming home from school and crying when she had to go again the next day. My wife and I wanted more information why she was so distressed. We learned from her that there were two classmates that she claimed were being mean.

"What are they doing?" we asked.

She said they smiled at her.

I said, "Well, that's nice."

"No, it's not," she replied. Apparently it was not a nice smile. Already at age six she was tuned into which smiles are nice and which are not. This is something I have yet to discern.

Something had to be done. Our daughter was so disturbed by these matters she was unwilling to go back to school. While she was there she was distracted away from her ability to learn.

At our evening prayer time before going to sleep, I set forth a plan for her. I asked her to do one thing every night at prayer time for just one week. If she would do this simple thing each night for seven days, then we would reevaluate and consider a change if needed.

She had identified two girls in her class who were her problem. I asked her to give thanks to God for these two girls just once a day for seven days. I told her what she is to speak out loud: "Father God, I thank you for Jane and Susan" (not their real names).

My daughter said, "I can't do that. I'm not thankful for them. They are mean to me. I would be telling a lie to God. There is nothing to be thankful for."

I told her it does not matter what feelings she has about this or whether or not she is sincerely thankful. All she has to do is say those words once a night for seven nights. She argued with me and would not say those words. So I said to her that she will then have to continue going to school with these feelings and we will not reevaluate after one week or consider a change of circumstances.

After a bit more persuasion she agreed to say this prayer just once per night for seven days. Oh, how she struggled to say those words, "Father God, (pause) I ... thank ... you for ... Jane ... and ... Susan." There was agony in her voice and contorted facial expressions as she forced out those words.

The next day at school was the same for her. She came home crying and disturbed about these two girls in her class. On the second night she said this prayer of thanksgiving again, this time with just a little more ease. Again she prayed the third night. On the fourth night, she was jovial and seemed to pray the same prayer from her heart.

I asked her then how things are going at school. "Good," she said.

"How is it with Jane and Susan?" I asked.

She replied, "Oh, it's good, we're best friends now!"

Relationships can be fickle for a six year old (and sometimes also for adults). I do not know what brought about such a change in circumstances. I do not know if the others changed or a change occurred in her. I was thankful for whatever the Lord had done.

THANKSGIVING REDIRECTS PERSPECTIVE

So many are slaves to their feelings, perspectives, and misplaced beliefs that are not subject to the Word of God. Our daughter was captured by her ill feelings toward these two girls. For what we heard from her during those days, she was unwittingly trying to also enslave us to her feelings.

When she was giving thanks to God for these two girls she was placing her will above her feelings, emotions, perspectives, beliefs, and relationships. She chose, with some parental persuasion, to say words in obedience to God despite the objections of her own soul at the time. When we give thanks to God in the Name of Jesus Christ FOR everything, this moves the heart of God. He may not change the outward circumstances the way we may wish for, but this opens our heart to the Father's heart. He will sooner or later work things together for His good purposes.

This is why we are told to give thanks *for all things*: because God works *all things* together for good. Rom. 8.28 says: "We know that God works all things

> *When we give thanks to God in the Name of Jesus Christ FOR everything, this moves the heart of God.*

together for good for those who love him and are called according to his purpose." We thank God for all things because God works all things together for good.

Father God is the Great Redeemer who transforms us and works His purposes to make all things new.[4] Giving thanks to the Father for the bad things of life does not ascribe responsibility to God for those things. Giving thanks for all things, including the bad things of this world, is a statement of faith that somehow and sometime God will work all things together for good.

This is why we are told to give thanks for all things: because God works all things together for good.

Thanksgiving has no magic that changes the past so it did not happen. Thanksgiving places trust in God and gives Him praise for whatever He will do. He will work all things together for good. "All things together" is a collective statement. That is to say, God's redemptive work fits into a larger plan that is good. The old things are made new, redeemed according to God's plan. So the alcoholic who becomes a Christian is able to empathetically minister to others going through the same trials. The one who suffered great loss because of thievery has peace inwardly and knows God as provider. The mistakes and failures of life are transformed into insights and guidance for the future. Give thanks to God for all things because He is the Great Redeemer who works all things together for good for those who love Him and are called according to His purpose.

It will feel strange at the first times you thank God for the disappointments of your life. Your mind and emotions will argue with you. Keep at it with perseverance. Watch what happens in your thinking and in your heart. The circumstances themselves may also somehow change as thanksgiving has released the power of God.

The Bible calls this a sacrifice of praise. Jonah spoke of a sacrifice of thanksgiving. This is when praise is not easy to do. Heb. 13.15 says: "Let us continually offer up the sacrifice of praise, that is the fruit of lips that give thanks to his name" (NASB). The sacrifice of praise is giving thanks to His Name. Note again that thanksgiving is given to the Name. We praise and give thanks to the *Name* of Jesus.

CEASED FROM SIN

I worked as a counselor at a Bible camp for two summers during my college years. At that time I had been a Spirit-filled Christian for a couple years. During the second summer at this camp I became attracted to one of the other female counselors. Over several weeks this attraction was mutual. So I was in a type of dating relationship with this girl. I was praying for her and with her, asking God to bless us in the Name of Jesus. I was aware in my heart that my desire for her became greater than my desire for God and His will. Though we did not enter into any outwardly sinful actions, my relationship with God was not right. Furthermore, the camp's staff guidelines were forbidding dating relationships between counselors.

This soon became a rather dark time for me spiritually. I prayed and read the Word of God but it seemed God was far away. After a couple months the camp director took me aside and reminded me of the responsibilities of being a camp counselor and the particular commitment to avoid dating relationships with another counselor.

There were other dynamics during that summer that added to the darkness I was experiencing. Another co-worker with whom I worked closely was from the opposite political perspective. This did not matter much to me, but she was troubled and struggled working with me. I also learned another male counselor was very disappointed in me and was sure to let others on the camp staff know of his disappointments. He spoke to me with such strong feelings about this. It caused me to wonder about his own motives.

I was painfully aware of my own contributions to the darkness that hovered over me during those months, but I was also learning of some of the enemy's spiritual forces also at work. The spiritual heaviness upon me at that time was oppressive.

I began to ask forgiveness from the Lord and repent, but there was no change. So I began to offer up a sacrifice of praise. I began to praise God and thank Him for the circumstances I was in. I was careful to thank Him FOR everything, good and bad, right and wrong, in my life. I was not blaming God, nor was I declaring Him as the author of the bad and wrong things. I was thanking God based on the promise that He will work all things together for good for those who love Him and are called according to His purpose.

I did not feel thankful. The words of thanksgiving I spoke were not heartfelt. They came solely from my will, choosing to do the Word of God despite my feelings and experiences. I could not conceive how any of this could work together for good. My faith was small. It seemed to me that I was just saying words that I was forcing myself to say. They did not seem to come from my heart which was wounded and confused. Nevertheless I persisted in giving thanks for everything in the Name of the Lord Jesus Christ to God the Father.

Summer merged into fall so summer camp ended and my senior year of classroom studies resumed. My roommate then also had had some trying circumstances for which he was seeking healing. So we opened our hearts to one another and to the Lord. There was no particular moment when I was suddenly released from this oppression. Rather over the course of a few months, with day by day fellowship, thanksgiving, and reading and memorizing the Word of God, I was restored to close fellowship with the Lord. The wounds and pains in my heart were gone. My eyes were opened and my perspectives were renewed. I was then able to look back on that past summer with heartfelt thankfulness for what the Lord had done in my life, how His mercy and grace was upon me.

Going forward, I was careful not to follow my emotions and desires especially in matters of dating. So when I had an interest or attraction to another woman, I submitted this to the Lord asking for His will, trusting His plans more than my own desires.

For the next four years I did not date anyone. This was not because I did not have attractions or interest; it was because every time, except once, the Lord said "NO" to me when I asked Him if I could pursue a dating relationship. The one woman who I did take to a movie during this time was actually a good friend I was not too interested in dating. So from age 21 to age 25 I essentially did not date. This was not because I did not want to be in a dating relationship; it was because I had the fear of God to obey Him above my own will.

When I was about 24 years old, after three years of no dating, I grew angry with the Lord who always seemed to say "NO." (I was going to say that I grew disheartened, a nice word. The truth is that I was angry.) One day as I was pulling into a parking lot in my car, I stayed in the car for a while and took some time to honestly and humbly express my frustration and anger to the Lord. I asked Him, "Why are you always saying 'NO' to every woman I had some attraction to?"

In the next moments as I sat in my car the thoughts began to form in my mind as I am sure the Spirit of God was answering me, "You don't know how much pain and hurt I have spared you and others during these years. Had you pursued those interests, there would have been complications and hurts for you and others." These words came to me bringing calm and peace to my heart.

About a year later, I met a woman at church whose name was Patty. I asked the Lord about her and the inner witness of the Holy Spirit was "YES." We were married a year and a half later and now, after 34 years, I am so thankful to God for her and how He works all things for good for those who love Him and are called according to His purposes.

> Since therefore Christ suffered in the flesh, arm
> yourselves with the same thought, for whoever has
> suffered in the flesh has ceased from sin, so as to
> live for the rest of the time in the flesh no longer by
> human passions but by the will of God (1 Pet. 4.1-2).

THANKS FOR EVERYTHING

Thank Him FOR everything. This goes beyond the things that we are already thankful for, as thanking God for the great many good things and provisions is easy. We must always make efforts to thank God for these blessings. But this verse says much more. Paul instructs us to ALWAYS and FOR EVERYTHING give thanks. These may be things we understand as good and for which we truly have a heartfelt gratitude. These are also things we do not understand, things we do not feel thankful for, even things that are malignant with trouble, people who persecute us, others who harm us, ones we do not get along with. Always and for everything means at all times for all things. This is more than giving thanks to God *in the midst of* or *in spite of* these undesirable circumstances. These words of scripture speak of giving thanks FOR everything in the Name of Jesus to God the Father.

This is not to ascribe blame God for the works of the devil who comes to steal, kill, and destroy. This is not imputing God for the consequences that come with wrong doing. To thank God for the bad things that come our way is not to make Him the author of these events or cast blame.

When you give thanks for something that did not come from God, you do so in faith that He will work it together for good. Thanking God for such things is not retroactive, but instead proleptic. Thanking God in the Name of Jesus for the good things is retroactive, looking back on blessings provided with gratitude. Thanking God in the Name of Jesus for the bad things is proleptic, looking ahead to thank Him in advance for whatever He will do.

This is the power of the sacrifice of praise. It is recognizing that He is the great Redeemer who is able to make all things new. He is the One who can bring the most painful thing in your life into a blessing. This is the power of praise. It is the sacrifice of praise, the fruit of lips that give thanks to His Name. We give thanks for all things, good and bad, because God works all things together for good for those who love Him and are called according to His purpose. We can thank Him for ALL THINGS because He works ALL THNGS together for good. We are thanking God for what He will do, for His redemptive plan and action.

THERE IS MORE

According to Eph. 5.20, even our praises and worship do not go directly to God. They come to Him in the Name of our Lord Jesus Christ. "Giving thanks in the name of the Lord Jesus Christ to God the Father." Col. 3.17 adds to this truth: "giving thanks to God the Father through him." Our thanks and praise to God the Father occurs in the Name of Jesus. Our thanks proceeds through the Son to the Father. Thank the Father in the Name of Jesus. Frequently say in all circumstances, always and for everything, "I thank the Father in the Name of Jesus."

Phil. 4.6-7 states another "in everything": "In everything by prayer and supplication with thanksgiving let your requests be made known to God. And the peace of God, which passes all understanding, will keep your hearts and your minds in Christ Jesus."

Pray and give thanks in everything. Thanksgiving and supplicant prayer causes your heart to stay in Christ Jesus. Thanksgiving that bypasses your understanding causes God's peace, which passes all understanding, to come to you. Give thanks in the midst of and for everything, as understanding or feeling thankful is unnecessary. Nothing is said in these verses of scripture about feelings, knowledge, or insight. The exercise of the will to thank the Father in the Name of Jesus for everything overrules insight, emotion, circumstances, beliefs and ritual. Thanksgiving is a primary strategy to acquiring and maintaining a transformed mind that abides in Jesus. God's peace is kept in your heart and mind. Giving thanks to the Father in the Name of Jesus is a powerful tool always available to us.

Chapter 15

ASK IN MY NAME

Some estimate that over 7000 promises are stated in the scriptures. Others tally the total to be over 30,000 promises. Among these thousands of great promises in the Word of God, standing out above them all is the incredible promise that we can ask anything in His Name and it will be done. This comprehensive promise is found in John 14.13-14: "Whatever you ask in my name, I will do it, that the Father may be glorified in the Son; if you ask anything in my name, I will do it."

In this great promise Jesus essentially gives His disciples a blank check. He says it once then He repeats the promise – "whatever you ask in my name, I will do it … if you ask anything in my name, I will do it." For Jesus to make such a promise implies a great amount of trust given to those whom He delivered this promise. It was Jesus's great pleasure to repeat this promise because He knew He would thereby bring glory to His Father.

The key to this promise is the Name of Jesus. Ask in the Name of Jesus in order that the Father may be glorified in the Son. What is it then to properly ask anything in His Name? How does the Christian believer confidently make such supplication?

This implies a relationship with the provider, God the Father. This relationship is only possible in Jesus's Name. Asking in Jesus's Name brings glory to the Father. Jesus repeated this great promise

146

because of the glory that He would bring to His Father when supplications are granted. Jesus's motivation for making this awesome promise was His desire to bring glory to His Father in heaven. So Jesus's great pleasure is to grant what you ask in His Name so that the Father may be glorified in the Son.

DOES THIS REALLY WORK? CAN THIS TRULY BE?

Everyone who has read these verses and decided to ask the Father for something in Jesus's Name will be able to testify how such prayers were answered as requested. Those same people will also report at least some instances when the things asked for in Jesus's Name were not given by the Father, at least not in stated the time frame or specific method or strategy. What about those times when things did not happen just as requested? Rather the opposite may have occurred. On the one hand, the words themselves are promises from Jesus and they build faith to believe in Him and put this promise to use. On the other hand, there may be some hesitancy, some questions, as this seems too good to be true and past attempts to ask in Jesus's Name did not always produce what was requested.

Virtually every believer has mixed thoughts about these verses because the results have seemed unpredictable. This easily becomes an opportunity for the devil to interject his lies. Like the temptation that came to Eve in the garden, Christians may be tempted with the question, "Did God really say that?" The battleground of our thoughts may produce other condemning conclusions such as "I do not have enough faith," "Those promises might work for others, but not for me," "God doesn't care about me," or "Something is wrong with me."

The key to this great promise, "ask anything in My Name," is the Name of Jesus, which shows the importance of understanding and asking of that Name. We may say the words "in the Name of Jesus" after a prayer, but may actually be asking the Father "in our own name," according to our own fleshly desires, seeking our own will instead of God's will. Asking in Jesus's Name is not asking in our name then attaching Jesus's Name at the end of the prayer, which is more of an abra-cadabra-like phrase to obligate God to do our will and request. When we try to give God our job description for Him, He does not do that job very well. This great promise does not make God our puppet for us to manage and manipulate. The key to this promise is understanding what it is to ask in Jesus's Name.

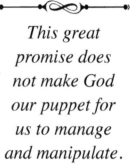

This great promise does not make God our puppet for us to manage and manipulate.

WE HAVE THIS CONFIDENCE

John spoke of a confidence we have before God that establishes effective asking and receiving. Look at the inspired Words of God recorded in John's epistle:

> Beloved, if our hearts do not condemn us, we have confidence before God; and we receive from him whatever we ask, because we keep his commandments and do what pleases him (1 John 3.21-22).

> And this is the confidence which we have in him, that if we ask anything according to his will he hears us. And if we know that he hears us in whatever we ask, we know that we have obtained the requests made of him (1 John 5.14-15).

But most Christians today lack this confidence. Many will offer prayers with hope, but little expectation of provision from God. Some pray with hope that something good will happen. Some do not receive from the Father simply because they do not ask. Others ask of the Father to spend it on their own passions. Many Christians ask of the Father God in the Name of Jesus and are not confident that God will grant what is asked.[1]

WE KNOW

John wrote about asking with confidence. John uses the phrase "we know" 16 times in the five chapters of his first epistle. "We know" exudes confidence. We know because of the certainty, the conviction, the faith that is worked in the hearts of believers in an abiding relationship with the Father through the Name of Jesus Christ. The Holy Spirit bears this witness of son-ship and daughter-ship in our spirits. This brings us to know that God hears us when we ask anything according to His will and know that we have obtained what is requested.

So there are conditions or stipulations involved when praying to the Father in the Name of Jesus. What are these conditions? Knowing this brings understanding of how to pray in the Name of Jesus from a position of confidence. These verses in 1 John have four qualifiers that give insight into asking in the Name of Jesus.

1. If Our Hearts Do Not Condemn Us.

The "heart," in this context, is not the physical heart that pumps blood. This usage of "heart" refers to the human conscience, our innermost being. "Heart" is synonymous with the human spirit. God has created us with this ability to feel and know guilt and condemnation. A heart that is self-condemning is a good thing - IF this leads to repentance and forgiveness. If a heart lacks repentance and forgiveness, it will continue in some amount of separation from God. A heart that condemns us should be viewed as a blessing if this will cause one to draw near to God to receive mercy and grace. When this grace abounds, "There is therefore now no condemnation for those who are in Christ Jesus."[2]

Yet so many believers live continuously in a guilt relationship with God, that is, each time God is approached in prayer, it is for forgiveness of sins. We can always come to Him to receive forgiveness, but for some the relationship never goes beyond this. Think about what it would be like to relate to another person this way. If your best friend only spoke to you about his sins and shortcomings and repeatedly asked forgiveness for them, but never realized you accepted him as he is and never discussed anything else, this relationship would be superficial, even tiring.

We can always come to Him to receive forgiveness, but for some the relationship never goes beyond this.

If there truly is a need for repentance and forgiveness, do not skip this necessary step, but do not get stuck there. "For godly grief produces a repentance that leads to salvation and brings no regret, but worldly grief produces death."[3] A relationship with God through Jesus Christ goes far beyond repentance and forgiveness. We must accept the truth that believers are made clean by the Word of God. "You are already made clean by the word which I have spoken to you."[4] So "there is therefore no condemnation for those who are in Christ Jesus."[5]

You are crucified with Christ. Your old nature died with Jesus on the cross. The Holy Spirit bears witness in your spirit that you are a child of God, an heir of His Kingdom. "Let us then with confidence draw near to the throne of grace, that we may receive mercy and find grace to help in time of need."[6]

2. If We Keep His Commandments.

The key to abiding in Him is to keep His commandments. Keeping His commandments brings confidence in prayer. 1 John 3.24: states: "All who keep his commandments abide in him, and he in them. And by this we know he abides in us, by the Spirit which he has given us."

Disregard of the commandments of God will separate you from Him, so that prayers spoken in the Name of Jesus are less confident. Our old nature does not want to obey God's commandments, but when we do obey we have confidence before God to ask anything in His Name.

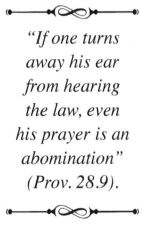

Keeping His commandments brings confidence in prayer.

The Old Testament scriptures contain over 600 laws the Hebrew people were to observe. They were routinely disregarding and violating these laws due to the weakness of the sinful human nature. This separated them from God and hindered their prayers.

> Behold, the Lord's hand is not shortened, that it cannot save, or his ear dull, that it cannot hear; but your iniquities have made a separation between you and your God, and your sins have hid his face from you so that he does not hear (Is. 59.1-2).

So disregard of God's commandments has a direct consequence for effective prayer. God's face is hidden from those persisting in unrepentant sin. He does not hear prayers couched in iniquity. Peter wrote in his first epistle, "For the eyes of the Lord are upon the righteous, and his ears are open to their prayer. But the face of the Lord is against those that do evil."[7] The book of Proverbs also has some very strong words regarding prayer:

"If one turns away his ear from hearing the law, even his prayer is an abomination" (Prov. 28.9).

"If one turns away his ear from hearing the law, even his prayer is an abomination."[8]

We now live under a better covenant, not dependent on our broken, sinful nature, but based on the work, the blood, the Name of Jesus who has imputed His righteousness into our being and has empowered us to live the Christian life by sending us the Holy Spirit. The multiple laws of the Old Testament are fulfilled in Him. The commandments are simplified and summarized in loving one another and believing in the Name of Jesus. "This is his commandment, that we should believe in the Name of his Son Jesus Christ and love another."[9] The commandments of God are offensive to one who is rebellious, but to one who submits to Him and His Word, the commandments are not burdensome, but empowering for life and effective prayer.

> For this is the love of God, that we keep his commandments. And his commandments are not burdensome (1 John 5.3).

3. If We Do What Pleases Him.

A third condition, for having confidence before God the Father in prayer, is doing what pleases Him. In order to DO what pleases Him we must KNOW what pleases Him. Many are unsure of what this involves. We may generate in our own minds what we think pleases God but if these ideas are not founded in the Word or God or if they come from a mind set on the flesh rather than the Spirit, God is actually displeased. "Those who are in the flesh cannot please God."[10] So what may please us or please others does not automatically please God. Desires of the flesh or self-pleasing desires opposed to God's will does not please Him and hinders confident prayer.

So we look to the Word of God to understand what truly pleases Him. Additionally, we understand what pleases Him by learning and knowing the voice of the inner witness of the Holy Spirit. How then do we do what pleases Him?

It begins with a desire and the choice to do what pleases Him, even before knowing exactly what does please Him. This is the fear of the Lord, the attitude of desiring to please God above pleasing ourselves or others. This is the position in which we can best know what does please Him. When we take delight in Him, He puts His desires in our hearts so we want what He wants. Ps. 37.4 states "Take delight in the Lord, and he will give you the desires of your heart." When we take delight in the Lord, He gives to us the desires of His heart. That is to say He puts His desires in our heart so our desires are His desires. So as a believer delights in the Lord the things he or she wants are the same things God wants.

He puts His desires in our heart so our desires are His desires.

Desires of the flesh and self-pleasing desires are opposed to God's will, but desires of the Spirit are infused into the one who delights in Him. This was the example of Jesus as He did not come to please Himself, but only to do the will of His Father. "For Christ did not please himself."[11] Therefore God was pleased with Him. "Thou art my beloved Son; with thee I am well pleased."[12]

Several other scriptures give us more instruction about what pleases the Lord:

> Without faith it is impossible to please him. For whoever would draw near to God must believe that he exists and that he rewards those who seek him (Heb. 11.6).

153

I will praise the NAME of God with a song; I will magnify him with thanksgiving. This will please the Lord more than an ox or a bull with horns and hoofs (Ps. 69.30-31, emphasis mine).

Children, obey your parents in everything, for this pleases the Lord (Col. 3.20).

Finally, brethren, we beseech and exhort you in the Lord Jesus, that as you learned from us how you ought to live and to please God, just as you are doing, you do so more and more (1 Thess. 4.1).

When a man's ways please the Lord, he makes even his enemies to be a peace with him (Prov. 16.7).

4. If We Ask According To His Will.

"This is the confidence which we have in him, that if we ask anything according to his will he hears us. And if we know that he hears us in whatever we ask, we know that we have obtained the requests made of him" (1 John 5.14-15).

A fourth condition, for having confidence before God the Father in prayer, is asking according to His will.

"Our thoughts and prayers are with you" – a frequent saying expressed nowadays when someone suffers loss of a loved one. I suspect for many it may simply be thoughts only. Perhaps some of these thoughts are directed toward God or about God. This scripture specifically calls us to ask. Asking begins with thoughts but is more than thoughts. Asking involves words that are spoken. Such prayer is a request that is uttered aloud.

I remember hearing a saying at Valentine's day, "It's the thought that counts." Does this mean I can simply think about my wife and think about a gift for her, then leave it at that? If I told her I thought about a gift for her, she would not be blessed. Rather she and any other woman would likely be offended. The thought alone does not count. If the thought is not completed with time and money to get her a gift, those kinds of thoughts are meaningless and ineffective, and probably offensive. "Let us not love in word and speech, but in deed and truth."[13]

Jesus said, "Ask and you will receive." Jesus did not say think and you will receive. It is not the thought that counts; it is the asking. Why ask aloud? Because you know when you have stopped. Our thoughts go on and on, but a spoken request of God in the Name of Jesus is a specific event.

James 4 says "You do not have because you do not ask."[14] Do not expect to receive from God if you do not ask from Him. He wants to give as He is the Lord our provider, but He wants us to come to Him with our requests, like a father whose daughter asks for some money as she has plans to go somewhere. The father then says, "OK, but come here first and give me a hug." Asking occurs in the context of relationship. This was the reason why God created us – to be in relationship with Him.

There is no expression of confidence before God if there is no request of Him. "In everything by prayer and supplication with thanksgiving let your requests be made known to God."[15]

But it is not just any request that comes confidently into God's hearing. The confidence we have is when we ask according to His will. Those petitions offered according to God's will come to His hearing and are

There is no expression of confidence before God if there is no request of Him.

155

granted. Spoken requests outside of God's will are excluded from this confidence we have before God.

So the key to this confidence is knowing the will of God. If we ask according to God's will, we know He hears us and we know that we will receive what we ask. This assumes we can know the will of God.

In our sin we do not accurately know God's will. Left to ourselves we cannot understand and know the will of God. Since Adam and Eve ate the forbidden fruit, they (and all people since) have knowledge of both good and evil. The problem is we do not accurately distinguish them. At times we may call evil good and good evil. All along we do so thinking we know the will of God. What may make perfect sense in our thinking and rationale is skewed and distorted because of a separation from God. "There is a way which seems right to a man, but its end is the way to death."[16] So the will of God is hidden and obscure due to our condition. God's will may not be what our thoughts, beliefs, experiences, preferences, or habits are predicting.

When Paul encountered Jesus on the road to Damascus, he was struck blind for three days until Ananias came to him. As Ananias laid hands on Paul to receive his sight, he spoke these words to Paul, "The God of our fathers appointed you to **know his will**, to see the Just One and to hear a voice from his mouth." (Emphasis mine)[17] Before this, Paul was convinced he was doing right by opposing, persecuting, and imprisoning Christians. Paul then came to know the will of God by revelation of the Holy Spirit. Thereafter his ministry was to proclaim the good news of the will of God in Christ Jesus to Jews and Gentiles. Paul wrote to the Ephesians saying this mystery was made known to him by revelation.[18]

Paul wrote to the Colossians about a man named Epaphras. He was servant of Christ who always remembered the Colossians earnestly in prayer. His prayer was that they would stand mature and fully assured in all the will of God.[19] How important it is to know all the will of God with assurance. This assurance is the confidence of asking the Father in the Name of Jesus according to His will. The will of God can be known so anyone can confidently ask of Father God in the Name of Jesus.

How do we discover and know with assurance all the will of God? His will must be revealed to us by the Word of God and the Spirit who brings revelation. The human mind must be transformed in order to know the will of God. The mindset that came as a result of eating from the tree of knowledge of good and evil must be redeemed and transformed..

This does not happen by engaging in more thinking, more rationale, or new philosophies. God does not usually transform us by appealing to our minds. He bypasses our minds to pour His love into our hearts. His appeal to us is to come to His throne of grace for mercy and forgiveness. His call engages our will to repent and submit our minds, our bodies, our souls to Him. The Spirit of God then begins to transform our minds to conform to the word and will of God. Jesus said, "If any man's will is to do his will, he shall know whether the teaching is from God or whether I am speaking on my own authority."[20] So we must set our will to do God's will even if we may not know what His will is. This is the attitude and approach in prayer that breeds confidence before God. This is denying self and determination to do God's will even BEFORE knowing what God's will is.

> I appeal to you therefore, brethren, by the mercies
> of God, to present your bodies as a living sacrifice,
> holy and acceptable to God, which is your spiritual
> worship. Do not be conformed to this world but be
> transformed by the renewal of your mind, that you
> may prove what is the will of God, what is good and
> acceptable and perfect (Rom. 12.1-2).

The will of God is a mystery revealed in Christ by the Holy Spirit. The Spirit of God speaks to our hearts to reveal the will of God and intercedes for us according to that will.

> And he who searches the hearts of men knows what is the mind of the Spirit, because the Spirit inter-cedes for the saints according to the will of God (Rom. 8.27).

> For he has made known to us in all wisdom and insight the mystery of his will, according to his pur-pose which he set forth in Christ (Eph. 1.9).

How then can we ask of God confidently according to His will? The mystery of God's will is revealed to us by the Spirit of God. This is always according to and consistent with the Word of God. We must get the Word of God into our hearts and minds so our hearts and minds are conforming to it and not to the world's ideologies. We must ascribe to and believe what God says in His Word. We choose to believe His Word over against the word of the culture, the words of the world, and also our own personal beliefs.

The will of God is recorded in the Word of God. Pray the Word. Get the Word into your heart and mind and pray accordingly with confidence. Set your will to do God's will, then let your requests be made known to God with thanksgiving in the Name of Jesus. "This is the confidence which we have in him, that if we ask any-thing according to his will he hears us. And if we know he hears us in whatever we ask, we know we have obtained the requests made of him."[21]

So the four conditions of confidence are: 1) if our hearts do not condemn us; 2) if we keep His commandments; 3) if we do what pleases Him; and 4) if we ask according to His will. When these four conditions are satisfied we have confidence before God.

These allow us to know that God hears us in what we ask. This is asking in the Name of Jesus. This is abiding in Him and God's word abiding in us.

> Therefore do not throw away your confidence, which has a great reward (Heb. 10.35).

> ...in whom we have boldness and confidence of access through our faith in him (Eph. 3.12).

> And now, little children, abide in him, so that when he appears we may have confidence and not shrink from him in shame at his coming (1 John 2.28).

> Through him you have confidence in God, who raised him from the dead and gave him glory, so that your faith and hope are in God (1 Pet. 1.21).

> In this is love perfected with us, that we may have confidence for the day of judgment, because as he is so are we in this world (1 John 4.17).

> If you abide in me, and my words abide in you, ask whatever you will, and it shall be done for you. By this my Father is glorified, that you bear much fruit, and so prove to be my disciples (John 15.7-8).

> Whatever you ask in my name, I will do it, that the Father may be glorified in the Son; if you ask anything in my name, I will do it (John 14.13-14).

> You did not choose me, but I chose you and appointed you that you should go and bear fruit

and your fruit should abide; so that whatever you ask the Father in my name, he may give it to you (John 15.16).

Truly, truly, I say to you, if you ask anything of the Father, he will give it wto you in my name. Hitherto you have asked nothing in my name; ask, and you will receive, that your joy may be full (John 16.23-24).

Chapter 16

GO IN MY NAME

We just reviewed the words of Jesus telling us to ask anything in His Name. What a great promise this is from Jesus! John's gospel provides additional insight as to how this promise works. There is a scriptural connection between asking and going in the Name of Jesus. Let's look at John 15.16. Note the words "so that" in this verse. It is the same as saying "in order that." This indicates a cause and effect relationship. That is to say, when one thing occurs it causes another thing to occur; because this, then that.

> You did not choose me, but I chose you and appointed you that you should go and bear fruit and that your fruit should abide; SO THAT whatever you ask the Father in my name, he may give to you (John 15.16, emphasis mine).

Jesus's words here say we are appointed and chosen by Him to go and bear fruit. When so doing, THEN whatever you ask the Father in Jesus's Name will be given to you. Therefore it is the going and bearing fruit that empowers asking in the Name of Jesus.

Most people are active, going here and there as part of regular daily activities that make up routines and necessities of life. So this call to us is to understand we are chosen by Jesus. Our election is to know the anointing that comes with the appointing. The challenge is to go in the Name of Jesus when going through the day's regular activities.

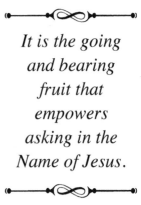

It is the going and bearing fruit that empowers asking in the Name of Jesus.

So there is a difference between going to the grocery store to get groceries and going to the grocery store in the Name of Jesus while getting groceries. How often do we go the grocery store for purposes of buying food? We can also go to the grocery story in the Name of Jesus. We can go and bear fruit when we go to buy fruit. That is, we can go there as His ambassadors with an ear toward Him for any divine appointments He may arrange. And while there pick up some groceries.

As you know, this applies to more than going to the grocery store. When we go anywhere in the Name of Jesus, we go with a purpose, with an awareness of being an ambassador for Christ, looking for and expecting divine appointments and opportunities to bear fruit. When Christians go anywhere in this way and bear fruit, then the Father will give whatever is asked in the Name of Jesus.

One of the youth directors I worked with had a theory. He said the farther you go from home on some mission trip, the greater God's anointing is upon you. This would seem to be true because of the prayers and preparations involved. There may be more boldness to speak and minister the gospel to total strangers compared with those interacted with regularly at home.

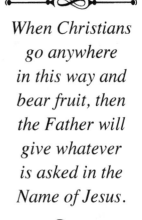

When Christians go anywhere in this way and bear fruit, then the Father will give whatever is asked in the Name of Jesus.

If there were the same amount of preparations and prayer, the same boldness and clarity of purpose, when going across your city or neighborhood, God's anointing is the same. This calling to go and bear fruit does not specify any specific distance or any amount of fruit. A special outreach or mission trip is going in Jesus's Name, but this need not be the only going. Our daily routines involve going.

GREAT TESTIMONIES

The next time you hear someone testify to an answered prayer, take note of any amount of going somewhere and bearing fruit as part of the testimony. Consider the one giving testimony of answer to prayer. Is there going and bearing fruit that abides in that person's life? Most likely there is, as the going and bearing fruit engages the truth in Jesus's words – SO THAT whatever you ask the Father in Jesus's Name, He may give it to you. Some of the greatest testimonies you will hear of God's provision are with those who go and bear fruit that abides.

Those who have left family and homes to go in the Name of Jesus are ones who have great power in prayer to ask in Jesus's Name. You have probably heard testimonies of missionaries who can tell many stories of answered prayer. These are people who have traveled far distances for extended lengths of time to bear the Name of Jesus Christ. But this promise from Jesus does not specify time or distance. It is simply going and bearing fruit that abides that empowers prayer. So if you go in the Name of Jesus across your city, across your neighborhood, across the street, even to another room in your own home, you have priority access to ask of Father God.

> Jesus said, "Truly, I say to you, there is no one who has left house or brothers or sisters or mother or father or children or lands, for my sake and for the gospel, who will not receive a hundredfold now in this time, houses and brothers and sisters and

mothers and children and lands, with persecutions, and in the age to come eternal life (Mark 10.29-30).

A CHAIR OF IMMOBILITY

When I attended college I took time every day to read the scriptures and pray. There was a rocking chair I commonly sat in during these times. Normally this was a rich time of prayer and scripture reading, but for several days this time was given to prayer about a dating relationship which was not going well at the time. I had been praying (more accurately I was complaining) about this matter to God, feeling sorry for myself, having a pity party all by myself. Surely no others would have wanted to join me in this pity party even if invited.

It occurred to me that this matter occupied my time, my thoughts, my heart. So I was somewhat paralyzed from following Jesus. My faith and calling from God were sitting there with me, immobile, resting in a chair. Instead of following Jesus, I wanted Him to follow me, my concerns, and my feelings. It became clear to me that I was sitting in this place emotionally, mentally, and spiritually just as I was sitting in that rocker physically.

A determination arose within me, a desire to leave that chair of immobility and pity. I wanted get up and go forth in the Name of Jesus. I spoke out loud as I got up from that chair, "In the Name of Jesus I'm leaving behind the pity and the heaviness. In the Name of Jesus I'm getting up to go and follow Him." A transformation occurred in my heart as I did so. The circumstances did not change, but my heart changed as I went forth in Jesus's Name. There was an inward change by going just a few steps in the Name of Jesus. The heaviness lifted; I stopped complaining; no more pity. Instead I followed Jesus. I went forth on that day in the Name of Jesus. There was no particular destination except to go about the business of the day. It was more about what I left behind as I proceeded through the day in the Name of Jesus, following Him in fellowship with Him, no longer in fellowship with my pity and complaints.

It is not the circumstances of life that hold a person from following Jesus and going forth in His Name, rather it is a matter of the heart and will. The circumstances, the trials, and tribulations control us only if we allow it. Jesus said, "in the world you have tribulation, but be of good cheer, I have overcome the world."[1] When we follow Him we participate in the faith that is the victory over the world.

It is not the circumstances of life that hold a person from following Jesus and going forth in His Name, rather it is a matter of the heart and will.

To follow Jesus involves going. Following Jesus is more than agreeing with His teachings. His disciples followed Him physically. They walked with Him wherever He went. Their actions came first, then they grew in faith and knowledge. As their footsteps followed along with Jesus's on His path, their understanding and insight of who He was took shape and grew. As they went forth in Jesus's Name, their prayers were empowered.

So get up from your place of grief, regret, sorrow, bitterness, anger, fear, and anxiety. Then go in Jesus's Name. Leave behind the things that entangle you and disable you, then choose in your heart and will to follow Jesus, His Word, His will, His Name.

This is the call extended to and required of anyone who would be a disciple of Jesus. "Then Jesus told his disciples, 'If any man would come after me, let him deny himself and take up his cross and follow me.'"[2] "Whoever does not bear his own cross and come after me, cannot be my disciple."[3]

GO THEREFORE

The Great Commission of Matt. 28.18-20 involves going. The last words of Matthew's gospel record are a great calling that exceeds beyond our human abilities. What did Jesus teach His disciples? He taught them to go, preach, teach, and heal. These were the same things Jesus Himself did.

> And Jesus came and said to them, "All authority in heaven and on earth has been given to me. Go therefore and make disciples of all nations, baptizing them IN THE NAME OF the Father and of the Son and of the Holy Spirit, **teaching them to observe all that I have commanded you**; and lo, I am with you always, to the close of the age" (Matt. 28.18-20, emphasis mine).

I took on a research project for the book of Matthew: how many times do at least two of these four activities (go, preach, teach, and heal) occur in the same verse? I was looking for verses that had both going and teaching, preaching and healing, or going, preaching, and healing, etc. I did not count those verses with just one of the four – I'm sure there are many. There were 35 such occurrences in the Gospel of Matthew. This gives insight to the Great Commission. Jesus taught and commanded His disciples to do what He was doing, namely to go, preach, teach, and heal. Matt. 4.23 and 9.35 describe Jesus's primary activities of ministry: "And Jesus went about all the cities and villages, teaching in their synagogues and preaching the gospel of the kingdom, and healing every disease and infirmity."[4]

Now His disciples are commissioned to teach all disciples the same things Jesus had commanded them: to go, preach, teach, and heal. This commission calls every disciple into doing some activities that are not humanly possible in our own strength. So Jesus promises to be with His disciples, with us, to the close of the age.

Every time the Word of God states the promise that God will be with us, it occurs in the context of some impossible tasks or circumstances, exceeding natural human capabilities. The Great Commission requires the Name of Jesus and the power of the Holy Spirit.

So Jesus also instructed His disciples to wait, to not go forth, until being clothed with power from on high. He told them to wait in Jerusalem until receiving the promise of the power of the Holy Spirit. Another Great Commission that establishes this truth is found in Acts chapter 1.

> But you shall receive power when the Holy Spirit has come upon you; and you shall be my witnesses in Jerusalem and in all Judea and Samaria and to the end of the earth (Acts 1.8).

It is the Holy Spirit who brings anyone to saving faith in Jesus Christ. No one can say, "Jesus is Lord," except by the Holy Spirit. After this initial profession of faith, a subsequent experience of the Holy Spirit is promised by Jesus. Believers are instructed to wait for the empowering of the Holy Spirit. Most commonly this occurs through prayer and laying on hands by another Spirit-filled believer.

After this empowering encounter occurs, believers are commissioned be witnesses in Jerusalem (your home town), Judea (your home state or country), Samaria (some area!), and to the end of the earth. The believers who gathered in the upper room received this power on the day of Pentecost. They were empowered and commissioned to go near and far. But they did not go forth, but rather remained in Jerusalem. Later a great persecution arose against the church. This caused the believers to be scattered throughout the region. It was persecution that caused them to go forth in Jesus's Name. Those who were scattered went about preaching the word, performing signs and wonders, so that multitudes believed in Jesus and followed Him.

Chapter 17

FIVE COMMISSIONS

We are considering the very important words of Jesus spoken to His disciples just before He ascended. These were words about continuing the mission in the Name of Jesus, about the commission to all disciples of Jesus to carry on His ministry in the power of the Holy Spirit. There are at least five scriptures that clarify this Great Commission. We should look at each one as together they capture the message Jesus left with His disciples just before He ascended to the Father. These five renditions of Jesus's commission are found in each of the four gospels and the Acts of the Apostles.

There are at least five scriptures that clarify this Great Commission.

And Jesus came and said to them, "All authority in heaven and on earth has been given to me. GO therefore and make disciples of all nations, baptizing them IN THE NAME OF the Father and of the Son and of the Holy Spirit, teaching them to observe all that I have commanded you; and lo, I am with you always, to the close of the age" (Matt. 28.18-20, emphasis mine).

And he said to them, "GO into all the world and preach the gospel to the whole creation. He who believes and is baptized will be saved; but he who does not believe will be condemned. And these signs will accompany those who believe: IN MY NAME they will cast out demons; they will speak in new tongues; they will pick up serpents, and if they drink any deadly thing, it will not hurt them; they will lay their hands on the sick, and they will recover" (Mark 16.15-18, emphasis mine).

Then he opened their minds to understand the scriptures, and said to them, "Thus it is written, that the Christ should suffer and on the third day rise from the dead, and that repentance and forgiveness of sins should be preached IN HIS NAME TO ALL NATIONS, BEGINNING FROM JERUSALEM. You are witnesses of these things. And behold, I send the promise of my Father upon you; but stay in the city, until you are clothed with power from on high" (Luke 24.45-49, emphasis mine).

On the evening of that day, the first day of the week, the doors being shut where the disciples were, for fear of the Jews, Jesus came and stood among them and said to them, "Peace be with you." When he had said this, he showed them his hands and his side. Then the disciples were glad when they saw the Lord. Jesus said to them again, "Peace be with you. As the Father has sent me, even so I SEND YOU." And when he had said this, he breathed on them, and said to them, "Receive the Holy Spirit" (John 20.19-22, emphasis mine).

But you shall receive power when the Holy Spirit
has come upon you; and you shall be my witnesses IN JERUSALEM and IN ALL JUDEA and
SAMARIA and TO THE END OF THE EARTH
(Acts 1.8, emphasis mine).

These verses contain the language of going in the Name of
Jesus. Along with the phrase "in My Name" we see words like
"go" and "send" and places like Jerusalem, Judea, Samaria, all the
world, and the end of the earth.

The combined message from these five renditions of Jesus's
commission to His disciples captures the call to go in Jesus's Name.
Viewed together the message is:

- Jesus has all authority.
- Before going, wait for the power of the Holy Spirit to
  come upon you.
- Disciples are to go everywhere in His Name.
- Baptize believers in the Name of the Father, Son, and
  Holy Spirit.
- Preach the good news to all creation.
- Teach other disciples to go, preach, teach, and heal.
- Signs and wonders will accompany you as you go
  in His Name.

DONDON, HAITI

In the mid '80s, I joined a short term mission team to the
country of Haiti. We traveled to a remote city named Pignon, a
Creole word we were told is pronounced "pee-on." (If there was
a university there, it would be Pignon U). At the time of our first
mission trip there, this particular town had no running water or
electricity. We helped build a hospital so the residents there had
another option besides the voodoo witch doctor. We returned the

next year to complete the surgical room of the hospital. There was now both running water and electricity in this community.

About six of us from this team took a day to travel about an hour to a more remote village named DonDon. This was a village tucked into a valley between two large hills or mounts. We got out of our vehicle onto wide dirt pathways that served as streets between the grass roofed huts. Our team leader had previously met the Pastor serving this village. We were visiting to consider offering help with construction, evangelism, and teaching.

We began to walk through this small village searching for this Pastor. Along the way we stopped at a few homes to present the gospel message and the Name of Jesus. Within ten to fifteen minutes of our arrival, the streets began to swarm with people. Before long a crowd of several hundred gathered around us in the street. We brought a brief message explaining the good news of the gospel, then set up two areas where people could receive prayer and ministry. Two long lines of people formed. One line was designated for accepting Jesus Christ as Lord as Savior; the other line was set apart for ministry of healing.

After several hours of ministry we spoke with this Pastor in his home. He had been evangelizing this community for years. When he had asked if any from this town of DonDon would like to invite Jesus Christ into their heart for salvation, the common reply was, "We will do so when the missionaries come."

We were those first missionaries to come to that village. We were the missionaries that came in His Name. Due to the preparations and preaching of this Pastor, the harvest was now ripe and abundant. What a great day of ministry, giving honor to the great Name of Jesus.

The Pastor was so grateful. Though he had very little, he insisted on serving us some food. He supplied some lettuce and fruit. These were foods we were advised not to eat in order to avoid food poisoning. We gave thanks in the Name of Jesus and ate without any adverse effects.

Chapter 18

SIGNS IN JESUS'S NAME

Let's look again at Jesus's Great Commission as recorded in the Gospel of Mark. After Jesus commanded those who follow Him to go into all the world and preach the gospel to the whole creation, He then uses His Name to describe what believers will do as they go:

> And these signs will accompany those who believe: IN MY NAME they will cast out demons; they will speak in new tongues; they will pick up serpents, and if they drink any deadly thing, it will not hurt them; they will lay their hands on the sick, and they will recover" (Mark 16.17-18, emphasis mine).

Jesus is commissioning believers to use His Name to do some specific actions. In the first parts of this book we explored what is the meaning of His Name. Here we continue with instructions from the Word of God as to how to use the Name of Jesus. Let's look at these in our effort to use the Name of Jesus according to the Word of God.

CAST OUT DEMONS

Years ago I was the leader of a young adult fellowship that grew to about 200 people regularly attending. We were led by the Holy Spirit to encourage special prayer and fasting for one week, then meet together to worship and give time for the Lord to do whatever He wills. (So often we plan events so rigidly that God is not given time to show up at the very events that we dedicate to Him.)

We met the next Tuesday evening and began to sing a song of worship. I had prepared three or four songs to start the evening. Part of the way into the first song, a woman in the front row began to tremble and shake. Soon she lost strength and fell to the floor as she continued convulsing. She was a beautiful woman who attended regularly and had good favor with everyone. All were surprised to see what was happening.

It was clear that the light of the presence and power of God exposed darkness. She needed us to drive out a demonic force that was now exposed and manifesting itself. This was rather easy to do as we had been praying and fasting for the past week and there were many praying, worshipping believers gathered there. A few of us laid hands on her and simply commanded the demonic presence to leave her in the authority of the Name of Jesus.

Within a minute she was set free. She recounted as we began to worship she felt this heaviness and ugliness upon her and shortly could not control herself. Then after driving out these forces she no longer felt this burden.

Many in developed countries do not believe in the existence of evil spirits or hell. I have taken note of a few news reports of surveys done over the years about whether people believe in the existence of hell or evil spirits. These surveys repeatedly indicate the majority in our culture believe in no such things. Yet we do not need to look far to see expressions of evil all about us. Every news report contains descriptions of wrongdoing by humans. Some of these tragedies are outright evil actions at the direction, inspiration, empowering, or control of demonic forces. Not believing in an unseen realm of darkness does not remove its presence. To ignore this conflict between the Kingdom of Light and the kingdom of darkness does not attend to the commission given to believers in the Name of Jesus. We need a biblical view of our country, not a cultural view of the Bible.

In the first chapter of Mark's gospel, just after He had called His disciples and had just begun His public ministry, Jesus drove out an unclean spirit.

> *To ignore this conflict between the Kingdom of Light and the kingdom of darkness does not attend to the commission given to believers in the Name of Jesus.*

And immediately there was in their synagogue a man with an unclean spirit; and he cried out, "What have you to do with us, Jesus of Nazareth? Have you come to destroy us? I know who you are, the Holy One of God." But Jesus rebuked him, saying, "Be silent, and come out of him!" And the unclean spirit, convulsing him and crying with a loud voice, came out of him. And they were all amazed, so that they questioned among themselves, saying, "What is this? A new teaching! With authority he commands even the unclean spirits, and they obey him." And at once his fame spread everywhere throughout all the surrounding region of Galilee (Mark 1.23-28).

This was the first sign and wonder among many others written in Mark's gospel account, recorded at the beginning in the first chapter. This event did not occur in the psychiatric ward or among the tombs. It was not in the pagan places of worship. It occurred in the synagogue of all places. Jesus's light came into the world and exposed darkness. This particular darkness was attending a worship service. So Jesus drove out the unclean spirit. It was a sign of His Messiahship, His anointing as the Son of God. Though we do not derive truth from demons, this particular unclean spirit spoke accurately as to who Jesus was and what He came to do.

There are at least five scriptures clarify this Great Commission.

Just as Jesus occasionally cast out demons to set people free, so will those who believe also drive out evil spirits in the Name of Jesus. Believers are given authority to cast out demons. This is a valid scriptural use of the Name of Jesus. Believers will expel demons in the Name of Jesus.

The believer's focus is not on demons, but on Jesus and His Name. There should not be a fascination with demons or that believers have power from the Holy Spirit to drive them out. However, neither should there be a neglect of the battle that believers are engaged in as victors

Believers will expel demons in the Name of Jesus.

over the works of the devil. "Be babes in evil, but in thinking be mature."[1] Simply stated, the Name of Jesus authorizes believers to cast out demons.

This is not a commission to take on all the forces of evil. Nothing is said in all of scripture about taking on principalities or the authority structures of the kingdom of the devil. Even the archangel Michael when contending with the devil did not pronounce a judgment, but left this to God. Believers are given authority over the power of the devil and to cast out demons. No scriptures confer authority to believers over demonic beings to pronounce judgment upon them. Daniel prayed to the Lord and did not himself take on the prince of Persia. The answer to his prayer was delayed three weeks as God sent the Archangel Michael to contend with this unseen principality.

Jesus has given authority to believers over the power of the enemy and to drive out demons. This does not authorize believers to take on the rankings of Satan's kingdom. Jesus's commission is focused on driving out demons from people to set them free. Though our battle is not against flesh and blood, but against principalities and hosts of wickedness in the unseen world of spirits,[2] believers are not granted a position to pronounce judgment upon them. The short book of Jude gives warnings about this.

> Yet in like manner these men in their dreamings defile the flesh, reject authority, and revile the glorious ones. But when the archangel Michael, contending with the devil, disputed about the body of Moses, he did not presume to pronounce a reviling judgment upon him, but said, "The Lord rebuke you." But these men revile whatever they do not understand, and by those things that they know by instinct as irrational animals do, they are destroyed (Jude 8-10, see also 2 Pet. 2.10b-13).

When Jesus commissioned the seventy disciples to go, preach, and heal, they returned saying that even the demons submit to them in Jesus's Name. Upon hearing this Jesus stated He saw Satan falling like lightning from heaven. These seventy drove out demons from some people who needed deliverance. In so doing there was an effect in the larger kingdom of darkness so Jesus saw Satan falling. These believers did not take on Satan himself. They did not challenge principalities or call down demonic archangels. Instead they did what Jesus commissioned them to do. They went, preached, and healed the sick. Doing these things in Jesus's Name had impact in the unseen spiritual world. So Jesus stated He saw Satan falling.[3]

SPEAK IN NEW TONGUES

Growing up attending a traditional Lutheran Church, I had never heard about speaking in new tongues except perhaps when the scripture was read on the day of Pentecost. I do not remember hearing any preaching or teaching about this.

In my first year of attending college I was part of a gospel outreach team that provided some special music at a Holy Spirit Conference. There were about 1000 people attending who worshipped sincerely and expressly with hands raised unto the Lord. My background in a small town at a stoic Norwegian Lutheran church did not afford me any such encounter in worship.

Between some of the worship songs there were a few that came to a microphone to speak some words of prophecy. I did not know these were words of prophecy and I did not pay much attention. Then another man came to the microphone and spoke in a new tongue. It was not like any human language I had heard before. After this message which no one could understand, the leader stated we have been given a message in tongues and now we should pray for interpretation.

Now God had my attention. This was a sign of something that I knew could not happen apart from the presence of God Almighty. This was a beautiful spoken language that could not have been manufactured spontaneously by a human mind. Now I wanted to hear the interpretation as I wanted to hear a message from God. So I prayed for this interpretation. This was perhaps my first prayer of wanting to hear from God. All of my prayers prior to this came from a motive of wanting God to hear me.

Before long another man approached the microphone and spoke words of interpretation we all could understand. The spoken words hit me in the chest. I knew this was a message for me, that God was calling me. The gist of the interpretation stated that the cleansing water of the Spirit avails for me and that I should repent and come to Him now before it is too late.

The return trip to my college campus was a seven hour drive. I had many questions about what I had experienced there. The others on this outreach team answered these questions very well with solid biblical answers. Several days later I knelt before the Lord in my dorm room to repent, ask forgiveness, and commit my life to God the Father through Jesus Christ.

This was speaking in new tongues in the Name of Jesus. It was a sign and statement to me which in turn brought me to saving faith in Jesus Christ and access through Him to Father God. Soon after repenting and committing my life to Jesus, I heard about the baptism of the Holy Spirit. I learned those who speak in new tongues do so by the presence, power, and inspiration of the Holy Spirit. I was given a book written by Mel Tari entitled "Like a Mighty Wind." This book was a record of amazing miracles happening in Indonesia. Therein was reference to the baptism of the Holy Spirit or being filled with the power of the Holy Spirit. I had not previously heard any preaching or teaching about this. It was easy to be open to this biblical truth as I had no previous negative baggage to overcome and I had seen powerful demonstrations of the Spirit's gifts and power working through believers at that conference. This is a promise from Jesus, a good gift from the Father.

I earnestly desired this gift along with all the spiritual gifts, any which ones the Holy Spirit would impart. I prayed fervently and took lots of time to put the Word of God into my heart. But for many months I did not receive this ability to utter new tongues by inspiration of the Holy Spirit. It was nine months later when I asked a Spirit-filled Pastor to pray for this gift for me. He laid hands on my head and prayed accordingly. I left the building and got into my car. When the door was closed and no one could see or hear me attempt to speak a new language, I opened my mouth and began to speak out words of a new tongue by the utterance of the Holy Spirit. I received this gift of speaking in tongues. Since then I use this gift every day in private prayer.

The scriptures state that he who speaks in a tongue edifies himself.[4] Every believer needs to be built up, to be edified in body, soul, and spirit. Jesus prayed for the Father to send the Holy Spirit including this particular gift.

The scriptures state that he who speaks in a tongue edifies himself.

It was about a ten minute drive back to my dorm room. The door to my room was open when I arrived. Inside the room was a rather casual friend. After an exchange of brief greetings, his next words to me were: "Have you ever spoken in tongues? I would like this gift from God if He would give it to me."

I do not remember how I answered him at that time. Just ten minutes prior was my first time to speak in new tongues. It was too awesome and fresh for me to tell him what had just happened. We talked a little about the promises of scripture about this gift and the empowering of the Holy Spirit. I was struck with the rather immediate divine appointment that occurred after receiving this special gift.

The next day I called this friend and told him what had happened to me. I boldly proclaimed to him that I could lay hands on him and pray and he will receive the same empowering of the Holy Spirit. We connected later that day where I simply repeated the same ministry that was effective for me the day before. The power of the Spirit of God visited him and he received this beautiful gift of speaking in new tongues.

The prophet Joel spoke of the days in which we now live. "And it shall come to pass afterward, that I will pour out my spirit on all flesh; your sons and your daughters shall prophesy, your old men shall dream dreams, and your young men shall see visions. Even upon the menservants and maidservants in those days, I will pour out my spirit."[5] This promise was fulfilled on the day of Pentecost and continues to this day and to the end of time.

Note the prominence of the Name of Jesus in Peter's inspired words. "And Peter said to them, 'Repent, and be baptized every one of you IN THE NAME OF JESUS CHRIST for the forgiveness of your sins; and you shall receive the gift of the Holy Spirit. For the promise is to you and to your children and to all that are far off, every one whom the Lord our God calls to him'"[6] (emphasis mine). This promise is to everyone called by the Lord, as a part of the Great Commission recorded in the books of Mark, Luke, John, and Acts.

Believers should earnestly desire this gift along with the other spiritual gifts listed in 1 Corinthians 12 and 14. Be sure of your resolve to follow Jesus and His Word. Seek out someone who has had an encounter with the Holy Spirit and His gifts. Ask this person to lay hands on you and pray for the impartation of the power and gifts of the Holy Spirit.

BY MEN OF STRANGE TONGUES

> In the law it is written, "By men of strange tongues and by the lips of foreigners will I speak to this people, and even then they will not listen to me, says the Lord" (1 Cor. 14.21).

About twenty people comprised a medical mission team to a small town called San Andreas. This was located about seven hours north of Guatemala City in the district of Quiche in the country of Guatemala. I joined this team made up of some who were medically trained and others who had no such training. Together we provided care to hundreds of people who were several hours away from any medical resources. As we met with each one, we asked if we could also pray for them. There were many opportunities to present the gospel and lead people to faith in Jesus Christ. But it was cumbersome because there were no interpreters who knew both English and the Quiche dialect. So we had two interpreters who translated from Quiche to Spanish to English and vice versa.

On a day of rest I was in need of exercise. (Sometimes our feelings of fatigue are our bodies in need of vigorous activity.) So I went on a run for a few miles. As I returned to the city, I was cooling down while walking the remaining few hundred meters to the orphanage where we were based.

As I came to the edge of the city, a man approached me as he was leaving the town. I stopped as he drew near and began to speak to him in tongues. He stopped and listened as I spoke what seemed like a few sentences. I did not understand anything I had spoken. However, it seemed as though he was understanding me. Then he spoke what seemed like a few sentences. Then I replied with more words I did not understand. I was not sure when to stop speaking and wondered if I might be cutting a sentence short. This conversation continued for a couple minutes, then I said a couple words I did understand. Earlier I had asked one of the interpreters how to say "do you understand?" in the Quiche dialect. So I asked him if he understood me. He nodded affirmatively.

What happened there was an encounter where the utterance given by the Holy Spirit brought some kind of word to that man. It was God speaking to a person by a man of a strange tongue and lips of a foreigner as recorded in 1 Cor. 14.21.

While on more than twenty short term mission trips to various foreign lands, I have attempted this strategy a couple dozen times. About half of these ended quickly as the others would often wave their hand and shake their head because they did not understand me. But the other half, about a dozen times, I found myself in a conversation that I did not understand, but the others did understand.

Speaking in new tongues in the Name of Jesus is a sign that will accompany those who believe.

For most people this gift of the Holy Spirit to speak in new tongues is a gift used privately in prayer and worship. Such prayer and worship bypasses the mind which does not comprehend what is spoken. But despite an unfruitful mind, speaking in tongues does strengthen and build up one's spirit. It is a great gift with great blessings. This is one way in which the Spirit intercedes for us according to the will of God.[7]

Speaking in new tongues can also be a form of public expression. A message may be spoken in an unintelligible tongue during the gathering of believers followed by an interpretation. This serves as a sign to unbelievers (as I was when I first heard this as described above). The interpretation essentially functions as a prophecy spoken to the assembled believers.

Some worship settings include a more free expression of worship where many will together sing and speak in new tongues. This is where believers gather to do in public what they may routinely do in private worship. It is not a message spoken to the whole assembly, but rather worship to the Lord Himself. No interpretation is necessary because the words are directed to the Lord in worship and not heard distinctly by others.

Yet another use of the gift of speaking in new tongues is as a tool for carrying out the Great Commission. Mark's record of Jesus's commission has the command to go into the entire world. Then Jesus states "IN MY NAME ... they will speak in new tongues (emphasis mine).[8] This use of tongues is what happened on the day of Pentecost when unlearned men spoke in the vernacular of foreigners visiting Jerusalem that day. These visitors heard these people extolling God in speaking their own native languages.

> And at this sound the multitude came together, and
> they were bewildered, because each one heard

them speaking in his own language. And they were
amazed and wondered, saying, "Are not all these
who are speaking Galileans? And how is it that
we hear, each of us in his own native language?
Parthians and Medes and Elamites and residents of
Mesopotamia,, Judea and Cappadocia, Pontus and
Asia, Phrygia and Pamphylia, Egypt and the parts of
Libya belonging to Cyrene, and visitors from Rome,
both Jews and proselytes, Cretans and Arabians, we
hear them telling in our own tongues the mighty
works of God."

Do you wonder why Luke takes time to list all of these people
groups? He does so to stress the amazing work of the Holy Spirit to
give utterance to unlearned men to speak in all these different languages. The most learned person with the greatest mental capacity
could not accomplish this feat.

How then is speaking in tongues a tool for carrying out the
Great Commission? Why would Jesus include this as a sign accom-
panying those who believe and go forth to all the world in His
Name? Because a commission to go into all the world with the
gospel message will be met with significant language barriers.
The power of the Holy Spirit, enabling believers to speak in new
tongues by inspiration and utterance given by the Spirit, can bypass
this barrier. "By men of strange tongues and by the lips of foreigners will I speak to this people."[9]

At the days of the building of the tower of Babel, the Lord said
that the people were one and nothing would be impossible for them.
So God confused their language so that they would not understand
one another's speech.[10] In their unholy unity nothing would be
impossible to them. How much more will nothing be impossible
with the holy unity among believers in the Name of Jesus Christ?
On the day of Pentecost they were united in the upper room, filled

with the power of the Holy Spirit, and spoke in many unlearned languages to declare the greatness of God. The sending of the Holy Spirit on the day of Pentecost empowered the believer's commission to go in the Name of Jesus Christ. This empowering included speaking in new tongues to advance the gospel message.

BE SAFE FROM SNAKES AND POISONS

> IN MY NAME ... they will pick up serpents, and
> if they drink any deadly thing, it will not hurt them
> (Mark 16.18, emphasis mine).

This verse was Jesus's supernatural guarantee that when going out on His commission, there would be divine protection against snakes and poisons. The commission of Jesus includes promise of protection from these environmental hazards which the enemy might try to use to stop or hurt them. This is not a commission to intentionally take up serpents or drink deadly things as a test of faith, but rather a statement of a particular protection from the Name of Jesus for those who go in the commission of the Name of Jesus.

For the disciples, it meant they were divinely guarded by the power of God. This divine protection was so powerful that even if they were to be bitten by a deadly snake or a highly venomous scorpion, it would have no effect on them. An example of this can be found in Acts 28:3-6 when the apostle Paul was bitten by a deadly viper. Paul simply shook off the snake into the fire and went away unharmed.

The Apostle Paul, who shook off the viper in the Name of Jesus and who went forth on missionary tours to proclaim the gospel of Jesus Christ, nevertheless met many trials, troubles, and tribulations. It was because of being shipwrecked that Paul had to stop at this island called Malta where he was bit by a snake. The storm at sea wrecked the ship but did not wreck Paul himself. Neither was Paul "wrecked" by the snake bite. This did not poison him. Paul was not spared from the effects of the storm at sea causing a wrecked ship, but he was spared from the deadly venom of the snake that bit him. Both of these circumstances enabled the gospel to come to the people of that island.

It is inaccurate to suppose this particular sign is a promise that believers are protected from all harm. It may be tempting to extrapolate from this verse that the Name of Jesus insulates believers from every kind of harm or danger. This verse makes no such promise. Rather, snakes and poisons were hazards that may occur when going forth in the commission of Jesus's Name.

There were and are many trials and tribulations for believers. The Apostle Paul's calling included suffering. When Ananias was to go pray for Paul to receive his sight, the Lord said to Ananias, "Go, for he is a chosen instrument of mine to carry my name before the Gentiles and kings and the sons of Israel; for I will show him how much he must suffer for the sake of my name."[11] Paul, who shook of the viper from his arm without any harm, was not spared from many other hardships. Paul wrote to the Corinthians:

> We are afflicted in every way, but not crushed; perplexed, but not driven to despair; persecuted, but not forsaken; struck down, but not destroyed; always carrying in the body the death of Jesus, so that the life of Jesus may also be manifested in our bodies. For while we live we are always being given up to death for Jesus's sake, so that the life of Jesus may be manifested in our mortal flesh (2 Cor. 4.8-11).

Later on in the same letter, Paul stated:

> Five times I have received at the hands of the Jews the forty lashes less one. Three times I have been

> beaten with rods; once I was stoned. Three times I
> have been shipwrecked; a night and a day I have
> been adrift at sea; on frequent journeys, in danger
> from rivers, danger from robbers, danger from my
> own people, danger from Gentiles, danger in the city,
> danger in the wilderness, danger at sea, danger from
> false brethren; in toil and hardship, through many a
> sleepless night, in hunger and thirst, often without
> food, in cold and exposure (2 Cor. 11.24-27).

But Paul did not suffer from snakes and poisons. Instead the snake biting him with no harm to him was a sign to the people of the island of Malta. At first they thought Paul was a god, but later brought many sick people to him for healing in Jesus's Name.

Jesus said trials and tribulations will come, but be of good cheer, "I have overcome the world."[12] We may not deal with serpents and scorpions like the early believers did, but there may be times when the Holy Spirit leads to places where we may fly on rickety airplanes, drive on dangerous roads, pass through highly volatile areas, or work in regions considered dangerous.

> Behold, I have given you authority to tread upon
> serpents and scorpions, and over all the power of
> the enemy; and nothing shall hurt you (Luke 10.19).

HEAL THE SICK

Healing and health is inseparably connected to the Name. "In my name...they will lay hands on the sick, and they will recover" (Mark 16.17-18). Supernatural healing from God comes through the hands of believers who understand the Name of Jesus. Healing power is released through the words of believers who abide in the Name of Jesus. Many accounts of physical healing occur when the Name of Jesus is spoken. This Name is the source of all health, wholeness, recovery, and well-being.

Fear His Name

The Word of God states healing is experienced by those who fear His Name. Mal. 4.2 states: "But for you who FEAR MY NAME the sun of righteousness will rise, with healing in its wings" (emphasis mine).

We hear much about how God's perfect love casts out fear. One can hear preaching about getting victory over various fears, as the Word of God promises. The Bible records the words "do not fear" a total of 77 times. But not all fear is bad. The fear of the Lord is desirable, protective, healing, bringing wisdom. The Bible records the words "fear the Lord" a total of 212 times, a three-fold emphasis.

At this time many have lost the fear of the Lord. Preaching about the love, mercy, grace, and forgiveness of God is the primary message of the gospel. But this does not exclude the benefits of fearing His Name. To speak of the grace of God without the fear of God is to attempt to remove the claws and teeth from the Lion of the tribe of Judah.

The word for fear is the same in all of these biblical references. "Do not fear" and "fear the Lord" have the same root word. Not all fear is bad. The primary witness of the scriptures prioritizes the fear of the Lord in a 3-to-1 ratio. Those who fear His Name will have the beginnings of wisdom, lack no good thing, be called friends of the Lord, have the Lord's eye on them, be encamped around by an angel, be blessed, and know the love of God.

We think of fear and love as opposites. God's perfect love casts out fear of other things. But it is the fear of God that brings us to experience God's love that casts out those fears. The fear of God brings us to know the love of God. If you do not fear God you will not know His love. A father's protective love for his child will include a firm discipline when needed. This is a clear message in several scriptures in the book of Psalms. Look at these two in chapter 113:

> For as the heavens are high above the earth, so great is his steadfast love toward those who fear him (Ps. 113.11).

> But the steadfast love of the Lord is from everlasting to everlasting upon those who fear him (Ps. 113.17).

Healing Witnesses to the Name

Which of the following three ministries brings the most threat to the devil's plans? A) someone who is saved by the grace of God and receives eternal life; B) a Christian who is baptized in the Holy Spirit's power; or C) the healing ministry of Jesus coming through a believer in His Name. Is it A) salvation, B) baptism of the Holy Spirit, or C) healing? Which one gives more trouble to the devil and thereby initiates more intense counterattacks?

Think of each one and what consequences it may bring to the kingdom of darkness. A soul that is saved is transferred out of the kingdom of darkness into the kingdom of His marvelous light. The primary front-line battleground in this life is for the souls of all people. This determines an eternal destiny in either heaven or hell. A favorite revival song has a phrase, "Jesus gained a soul and Satan lost a good right arm."[13]

The second one is when a believer is empowered by the Holy Spirit. This is the same power that raised Jesus Christ from the dead, the resurrection power of Jesus that comes to dwell with immeasurable strength in believers.[13] Greater is He who dwells in believers than he who is in the world.[14]

The third one is when a believer ministers physical healing to another person whose body is then healed in the Name of Jesus. This occurs when a believer learns to do what Peter and John did at the gate called Beautiful where the paralytic came daily. Peter said he did not have any silver or gold, but he would give him what he did have. Though Peter and John had no material things to give, they knew they had healing to give him. They also knew how to give healing to the paralytic. When a believer effectively ministers healing to another, there is an awareness of what he or she has to give and how to give it, just as Peter and John demonstrated.

Which of these three causes more consequences to the kingdom of darkness and therefore invites the most intense spiritual battles? The devil will attempt to attack those who are doing any of these three ministries. Which one disturbs the devil the most and may generate greater opposition from him?

Each one does. When a person is saved, filled with the Holy Spirit and healed of disease the kingdom of God advances and rejoices. The motivation for these ministries is done out of obedience to the great commission of Jesus, not simply to disturb the devil.

The question again is what ministry disturbs the devil most. The possible answers are A) salvation, B) baptism of the Holy Spirit, or C) healing. Of course, each of these three advances God's Kingdom and takes away from the devil's kingdom. Which of these has the greatest impact in battle between these two kingdoms and can be the front line of spiritual warfare? My answer to this question is C) healing ministry. Healing of the physical body is only a temporary blessing as our earthly bodies will be transformed to be like His glorious body when we enter the commonwealth of heaven. Even so, healing of this earthly physical body disturbs the devil the most. Here is why I think so.

Effective ministry of healing in Jesus's Name is predicated on the other two. Those who minister healing in Jesus's Name have believed in Jesus for their own salvation and have been empowered by the Holy Spirit.

All who believe and trust in Jesus and call upon Him will inherit eternal life, but some of these believers have not experienced the empowering of the baptism of the Holy Spirit. There are other believers who are so empowered, but do not learn to release the power within them to advance God's Kingdom according to Jesus's commission. Some believers are not aware of the great power within them or how to release it for healing.

Many believers who are assured of their salvation and empowered by the Holy Spirit do not understand what Peter and John did when they brought healing to the paralytic. Peter said, "I give you what I have." He knew what he had and how to give it. A Christian who ministers healing is releasing God's power to further the Kingdom of God. Such a person knows this resurrection power within and knows how to release this power for healing. This poses a great threat to the kingdom of darkness. When the seventy returned to Jesus with reports of healing, it was then Jesus saw Satan falling like lightning from heaven.

Furthermore, healing in the Name of Jesus is an unforgettable event that calls that person to abide in Him. It is a demonstration of the nearness of the Kingdom of God. This serves to confirm the message of the gospel. Such signs and wonders accelerate and override the efforts of proclamation and persuasion. A testimony of healing speaks to others on a different level than persuasive theological tenets. Theologies can be argued but a testimony or demonstration of the power of God cuts through arguments and philosophies.

A supernatural healing event is indelibly etched in the minds and memories of the one who received healing and the one(s) ministering healing in Jesus's Name. The one who ministers the healing

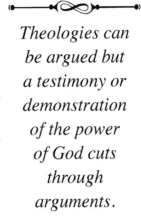

Theologies can be argued but a testimony or demonstration of the power of God cuts through arguments.

has come into a relationship of discipleship with God the Father with a confirmation of that calling and election.

A supernatural healing in Jesus's Name testifies powerfully to others. This testimony endures and is repeated sometimes for many years bringing glory to God and bringing others to faith in Jesus and His Word.

This greatly disturbs the devil's schemes, to lose a soul who had been following him. That believer will instead go forth in Jesus's Name in the great commission, demonstrating with signs and wonders the truth of the Word of God and the nearness of the Kingdom of God, bringing the good news to many others who in turn believe in Jesus for salvation.

THE PROMINENCE OF HEALING

This topic of healing occupies almost 20% of the scriptures in the four gospels of Matthew, Mark, Luke, and John. Jesus's ministry on earth was characterized by certain activities. He went about the region preaching the gospel of the Kingdom, teaching in the synagogues and healing every disease and every infirmity. Then He commissioned His disciples to the same things He was doing. Then they were commissioned to disciple others to do the same things that He taught them, that is, to go, preach, teach, and heal.

It seems there is more struggle and controversy that surrounds effective healing ministry in Jesus's Name. Among many Christians, Christian leaders, and theologians there is disagreement and disbelief regarding the promises of healing from the scriptures. Whereas the message of salvation is central to evangelical churches and such preaching is expected and not contested; and whereas the message of the baptism of the Holy Spirit is characteristic of charismatic and Pentecostal churches; the ministry of healing is often met with questions, skepticism, or dismay even among some Christians. This "battle" is not of flesh and blood, but is generated by forces of darkness with attempts to discredit and dismantle such ministry and anyone who attempts to minister the gospel with such signs and wonders.

There is much to consider and discuss regarding this usage of the Name of Jesus for healing the sick. I recommend you check out my book, "This Mountain", for more in depth discussion of the authority of the believer to heal the sick.

BRUCE'S SHOULDER

When believers gather together for worship and the word, there are songs ABOUT the Name of Jesus and there is preaching ABOUT the Name of Jesus. This is a great setting to also USE the Name of Jesus for His glory. At my church every two or three months we devote the Sunday morning services to physical healing in the Name of Jesus. We do not just talk about this, we do it, and with large response from our congregation. So many people everywhere need healing. We see many healings happening instantly and many others over some time. We are also waiting and persisting in prayer for others for whom nothing physical has happened yet.

(With so many people in need of healing and so many scriptures devoted to Jesus and His disciples ministering healing to others, it is curious that most churches might only talk and sing about this, but do not use the Name of Jesus with laying on of hands and word of command for healing. With almost 20% of the verses in the four gospels of Matthew, Mark, Luke, and John telling of stories of healing and teaching about the ministry of healing, it is a wonder that there is little time or opportunity for the those needing healing to come to the church for this ministry.)

After preaching at one of these healing services, I asked Father God to stretch forth His hand to heal the sick. I called for anyone to come forward who was currently having shoulder pain with or without decreased range of motion. There were five or six people who came to the front of the assembly. All of them had shoulder pain and most of them were unable to raise their arm above 90 degrees. Bruce was one of those who took the steps of faith to come in front of the congregation to seek healing from Jesus. He had right shoulder pain and was unable to raise his arm above his shoulder.

As many in our church have learned to do, I briefly laid my hand on his shoulder and spoke in the Name of Jesus directly to his shoulder. Jesus taught us to have faith and say to the mountain, "move from here to there," and it will move.

So I did just that, speaking words something like this: "In the Name of Jesus, I speak to the ligaments, tendons, bones, and cartilage in Bruce's right shoulder to be healed. I command the tendons to function normally. I release the tendons from any impingement from surrounding structures. I command the pain to leave in the Name of Jesus."

Then I said to Bruce, "Raise your arm up in the Name of Jesus." He did so without pain. He was able to move his shoulder in every normal direction without any pain. Glory to God!

Not only was Bruce healed, the whole gathering of people in church that day saw what Jesus did. He has given us the Name of Jesus for us to USE to His glory. All but one of those with shoulder pain and decreased range of motion were healed instantly that day. The next day Bruce contacted me, asking if I thought it would be okay for him to play tennis. He was not having any pain and had normal use of his right shoulder and arm. "Go ahead," I said. He continues with normal shoulder function free of pain. Glory to Jehovah Raphah, the Lord our Healer.

Those who abide in the Father through His Son Jesus and who properly understand and use the Name of Jesus will have signs and wonders that accompany them. They will speak in new tongues, they will cast out demons, they will heal the sick, and if encountering snakes or poisons they will not be harmed.

Chapter 19

DO EVERYTHING

And whatever you do, in word or deed, do everything in the name of the Lord Jesus (Col. 3.17).

We have discussed the expressions of giving thanks in the Name
of Jesus and asking the Father in the Name of Jesus. These
actions are spoken words. We have been given the Name of Jesus
for us to speak audibly. So we can SAY His Name, but we also can
DO His Name. Our deeds, every one of them, are to be done in
the Name of Jesus. Jesus stated even a cup of water given in His
Name brings a reward. So whatever is done, if done truly in the
Name of Jesus, understanding and acting according to His Name,
has benefit and reward. This is an act of doing that does not require
saying the Name of Jesus.

WORDS NOT REQUIRED

You can say the Name and you can do the Name. Words are
not always necessary when doing the will of the Father in Jesus's
Name. In Matthew's summary of Jesus's ministry as cited in 4.23
and 9.35, Jesus did four main activities: He went, preached, taught,
and healed. The preaching and teaching involved words, the healing
often involved speech, though sometimes Jesus healed by touch
only. His going did not require words.

Jesus did many miracles as a witness to the nearness of the Kingdom of God. He answered the Jews by saying, "The works that I do in my Father's Name, they bear witness to me."[1] Whatever Jesus did, He did so in His Father's Name.

Now take note of this: When Jesus did these works, there is no record of Him actually saying the words "in My Father's Name." Jesus did everything in His Father's Name but no scripture records Him attaching this spoken phrase to those works.

> So the Jews gathered round him and said to him, "How long will you keep us in suspense? If you are the Christ, tell us plainly." Jesus answered them, "I told you, and you do not believe. The works that I do in my Father's name, they bear witness to me; but you do not believe, because you do not belong to my sheep" (John 10.24-25).

Most prayers prayed by Christians end with saying the phrase "in the Name of Jesus." The Word of God teaches us to ask in the Name of Jesus. For most praying Christians, this involves adding the phrase "in the Name of Jesus" to every prayer.

THE APOSTLE'S USE OF JESUS NAME

But does this capture the full intent of using Jesus's Name? We see that Jesus did His works in His Father's Name, but is never recorded saying "in the Name of My Father" when He prayed or worked miracles. Let's look then at Jesus's apostles and disciples. How did they use the Name of Jesus? The book of the Acts of the Apostles gives us the best account of their works as they carried on the ministry after Jesus's ascension.

They were doing everything in the Name of Jesus. How then did they use His Name? They were not ashamed of the Name. They suffered because of the Name. They honored and proclaimed the

Name of Jesus. They preached and taught the good news of the gospel of Jesus Christ.

When ministering healing or other signs and wonders, did any of the apostles say the phrase "in the Name of Jesus?" Yes they did, but only recorded twice. Of all the miracles and healings recorded in the Acts of the Apostles, the words "in the Name of Jesus" were included only twice. The first was when Peter and John healed the paralytic at the gate called "Beautiful." "I have no silver and gold, but I give you what I have; in the name of Jesus Christ of Nazareth, walk."[2] The other occasion was when Paul drove out a spirit of divination from a slave girl. Paul said, "I charge you in the name of Jesus Christ to come out of her."[3]

They did everything in the Name of Jesus including preaching, healings, signs and wonders. They prayed that wonders would be performed through the Name of Jesus.[4] However they did not always attach the spoken prepositional phrase "in the Name of Jesus" when doing these works. Apparently this was not necessary or required as they were abiding in the Father through Jesus, they had confidence because their hearts did not condemn them, they kept His commandments, and they did what pleased Him. This is doing everything in the Name of Jesus.

ATRIAL FIBRILLATION

It is not uncommon in any Emergency Department to attend to a condition called Atrial Fibrillation. A person with this heart rhythm has an irregular rhythm and sometimes the rate is inappropriately accelerated. A man about 60 years old came in with this type of rhythm. His EKG showed Atrial Fibrillation with a resting heart rate at around 140 beats per minute. An IV was inserted so he could receive a medication called Diltiazem. This usually controls the rate and sometimes, but rarely, corrects the rhythm back to a normal sinus heart rhythm. After receiving this medicine his rate reduced to about 80 bpm but he continued in Atrial Fibrillation. When this medication wears off he would likely resume a rapid rate.

He was a candidate for synchronized electrocardioversion which is an electrical shock to reset or restart the heart. This is usually effective to return to a normal rhythm and rate. He agreed to this and was then sedated. A synchronized jolt of 150 joules of energy was delivered. His heart was reset as expected and returned to normal sinus rhythm – for about a minute only. Then he returned to the previous irregular rhythm. So while he was still sedated he received a second shock at 175 joules. Again he returned to a sinus rhythm for about a minute then back to a rapid Atrial Fibrillation.

This man had kidney failure and received dialysis three times weekly. Typically we hospitalize these patients, but we do not have inpatient dialysis where I work so he would need to be transferred elsewhere. While thinking he would likely need to be transferred and while he was yet unconscious, I put my hand over his heart. There were two nurses in the room also when I simply said, "I speak to this heart and tell you to stop fibrillating and return to normal sinus rhythm." These nurses did not know what I was doing, but I do not think they thought it was strange. I did not include the words "in the Name of Jesus" like I would typically do in a ministry encounter.

I went back to my desk to dictate documentation and move on to another patient. In about five minutes a nurse said he is displaying some normal beats in the midst of ongoing Atrial Fibrillation. Over the next 5-10 minutes he had more and more normal beats and returned to normal rate and rhythm. He was discharged home to continue his current plans. Glory to God.

Reflecting on this event, a few things are remarkable to me. In matters of health and healing, the natural and supernatural are often blended. God works through our strategies and treatments that involve tools and medicines. He also works supernaturally to intervene through believers apart from our tools and medicines. The natural and supernatural are both natural to God. There is often some mystery and unknowns about what exactly the Lord is doing when He heals.

After unsuccessfully attempting the normal treatment protocols for rapid Atrial Fibrillation, it seems the Lord restored his normal heart rhythm through laying on hands and word of command. I did not include the phrase "in the Name of Jesus" when I spoke to his heart. Jesus said, "If you have faith as a grain of mustard seed, you will say to this mountain, 'Move from here to there,' and it will move."[5] This mustard seed faith is the profound faith in the Name of Jesus, but these instructions do not include saying the phrase "in the Name of Jesus." This is simply doing in the Name of Jesus. Such doing comes from an abiding faith relationship in Him rather than simply saying some words.

The natural and supernatural are both natural to God.

NOT HUMAN DOINGS

The list of tasks that any given day brings can be fully occupying. Tasks to do at home, at work, hobbies, and projects demand our time and even our soul. Who we are can be defined by what we do, fail to do, or choose not to do. Though our days are filled with such busy-ness, this is not the sum of God's plan for His followers. His view of His people is not derived by what we do or do not do. He transforms our being, our identity, our inner nature and positions us in certain realms of authority. This happens before the believer does anything worthwhile, for apart from Him we can do nothing that is fruitful.[6] Our being is not based on our doings. Our doings come from our being. Who we are

Our being is not based on our doings. Our doings come from our being.

is defined and empowered by a relationship with the Father in heaven through His Son Jesus Christ.

When a person believes in Jesus for eternal life, he is a new creation, the old has passed away. The new has come.[7] Therefore what that person does comes from his new being in Christ. What we do comes best from who we are. The Christian embarks on a process of knowing who God is, who His Son is, and who the Holy Spirit is. This in turn brings revelation to who self is. We discover who we are when we receive revelation as to who Jesus is and what He has done for us. Such insight comes only by revelation from the Holy Spirit and the Word of God, not by introspection, personality inventories, or other's opinions.

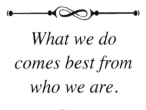

What we do comes best from who we are.

We must embrace and believe what God says about us. To do otherwise is a misconception of this new identity in Christ. The accuser of the brethren, the devil, makes this his primary scheme – to distort the true identity of the believer and discredit the Name of Jesus.

How many people confess untruths about themselves? How many, who are believers in Jesus Christ, are also yet making a wrong confession about self? Our self-perceptions, thoughts, confessions, and inner voice need to be transformed to agree with what God says who we are. Accepting anything short of God's declaration of who we are is unbelief and agreeing with the accuser.

We find these truths in the Word of God. We confess these truths with our mouths and choose to believe them in our hearts. This is an ongoing process of discovery as the believer grows in faith and understanding of the Word of God. Then what we do comes from who we are in Christ. This is doing everything in the Name of Jesus Christ. This doing comes out of a new being.

The focus of the devil is to distort these truths about who God is and who we are in Him. Behind sinful actions are ones who disbelieve, neglect, or forsake their identity as revealed the Word of God and by the Holy Spirit. We are not called "human doings," we are "human beings." So what we do comes out of who we are. For those delivered from the kingdom of darkness into the marvelous light of God's Kingdom, the doings come from a new identity in Christ.

The best preaching and teaching from the Word of God focuses on who the triune God is and who we are in Him. But hearing preaching that focuses instead on the dos and don'ts is rather common: do more good things and don't do the bad things; if you are praying 10 minutes a day, that is good, but now commit yourself to praying 20 minutes a day; if you are praying 20 minutes a day, you should be praying 30 minutes a day. Doing more and more becomes a heavy burden. The focus is more on what we do than what God has done for us.

> These have indeed an appearance of wisdom in promoting rigor of devotion and self-abasement and severity to the body, but they are of no value in checking the indulgence of the flesh (Col. 2.23).

HEARING ONLY

Some may not ever do anything in the Name of Jesus. It is not that nothing is done whatsoever, but whatever is done is not done in His Name. Many things can be done, but done so in some other name, for some other purpose, to please self or someone else. Such people may be hearing a message of the times, seeking the American dream, following personal desires and passions.

Others may use the gifts of the Spirit, drive out demons, and perform miracles while saying the Name of Jesus. Yet if these works are not coming from a knowledgeable relationship with

Jesus and not doing the will of the Father in heaven, they are not works truly done in His Name.

> Not everyone who says to me, "Lord, Lord," shall enter the kingdom of heaven, but he who does the will of my Father who is in heaven. On that day many will say to me, "Lord, Lord, did we not prophesy in your name, and cast out demons in your name, and do many mighty works in your name?" And then I will declare to them, "I never knew you; depart from me you evildoers" (Matt. 7.21-23).

These are strong words from Jesus. Those who do not do the Father's will, even when doing the same things Jesus did (prophesying, casting out demons, and many mighty works), are labeled as evildoers. They are not just misguided or uninformed, they are evildoers. Simply calling on the Lord and saying the Name of Jesus is not automatically a ticket to enter the kingdom of heaven. This is true even for those who do many mighty works while saying His Name. If doing does not come out of being in an abiding relationship with the Father through Jesus, then there is no true being from which the doing occurs. Here Jesus is saying that fruitful doing comes from an obedient relationship with God. This relationship comes from hearing and believing the gospel message of access to the Father through faith in His Son Jesus.

Fruitful doing comes from an obedient relationship with God.

Some of these people may also hear the Word of God without doing that same Word. When Paul instructed, "Whatever you do, in word or deed, do everything in the Name of the Lord Jesus,"[8] he was speaking about doing the Word of God. Doing everything in the Name of the Lord Jesus Christ is to be a doer of His Word.

> James 1.22-25: But be doers of the word, not hearers only, *deceiving yourselves*. For if anyone is a hearer of the word and not a doer, he is like a man who observes his natural face in a mirror; for he observes himself and goes away and at once forgets what he was like. But he who looks into the perfect law, the law of liberty, and perseveres, *being no hearer that forgets but a doer that acts*, he shall be blessed in his doing (James 1.22-25, italics mine).

Note that those who hear the Word without doing the Word are self-deceived. To hear the Word, believe the Word, accept the Word, embrace the Word, but not DO the Word, this will bring self-deception. To hear the Word and do the Word in Jesus's Name brings revelation and insight, blessings and reward. A hearer only of the Word will soon forget that Word. A doer that acts remembers the Word that is obeyed. A doer of the Word acts on that Word in Jesus's Name and is blessed. Doing the Word brings clarity to one's calling, purpose, election, and identity.

Those who DO in Jesus's Name will find that His words are true. "If any man's will is to do his will, he shall know whether the teaching is from God or whether I am speaking on my own authority."[9] So revelation knowledge comes, not primarily by study and mental exercises, but by wanting to DO the Father's will.

> *Those who DO in Jesus's Name will find that His words are true.*

WISE OR FOOLISH?

Wisdom is defined by doing. The wise man hears and does; the foolish man hears and does not do. Both hear; only one does.

Every one then who hears these words of mine and does them will be like a wise man who built his house upon a rock and the rains fell, and the floods came, and the winds blew and beat upon that house, but it did not fall, because it had been founded on the rock. And every one who hears these words of mine and does not do them will be like a foolish man who built his house upon the sand; and the rain fell, and the floods came, and winds blew and beat against that house, and it fell; and great was the fall of it (Matt. 7.24-27).

According to these words of Jesus, those who are wise are defined not by what is known or has been heard, but by what is done. The foolish are defined here not by lack of knowledge or education or training, not even by what is said, but by what is not done or is done wrongly.

Do everything in the Name of Jesus. Be wise by hearing His word, doing His word, and doing everything in His Name. Obedience to the Word of God is defined not by what a person says, but by what is done. The parable of the two sons clarifies this definition:

What do you think? A man had two sons; and he went to the first and said, "Son, go and work in the vineyard today." And he answered, "I will not;" but afterward he repented and went. And he went to the second and said the same; and he answered, "I go, sir," but did not go. Which of the two did the will of his Father?" They said, "The first." Jesus said to them, "Truly, I say to you, the tax collectors and the harlots go into the kingdom of God before you. For John came to you in the way of righteousness, and you did not believe him, but the tax collectors and the harlots believed him; and even when you saw it, you did not afterward repent and believe him" (Matt. 21.28-32).

Paul explained how he lived this out in Gal. 2.20: "I have been crucified with Christ; it is no longer I who live, but Christ who lives in me; and the life I now live in the flesh I live by faith in the Son of God, who loved me and gave himself for me." Paul considered himself dead to self and alive to God, so that everything said and done came from his faith in the One who loved him. Paul viewed his redeemed life as a life that was given him by God. It was no longer Paul who lived but God's Son Jesus who lived in him because He gave His life for him. So everything spoken and performed is done in the Name of Jesus.

DO EVERYTHING IN THE NAME OF JESUS

Most of us can look back over our lives and recognize that certain decisions were made or things were said and done that we now wish had been said or done "in the Name of Jesus." Many live with such regrets. If only these certain consequential deleterious actions had not been said or done, but rather something else truly done in the Name of Jesus. Perhaps at the time it was a matter that was prayed about and the words "in the Name of Jesus" were invoked, but looking back it becomes clear that it was instead it was actually done in the name of yourself or some other person, serving wishes and desires that were selfish rather that God's will.

But with repentance and forgiveness these same regretful missteps are redeemed in Jesus's Name. He is the great Redeemer. He works all things together for good. Even things said or done mistakenly are redeemed to work together for good, for those who love Him and are called according to His purpose.[10]

Paul wrote instructions to the Colossian believers: "Whatever you do, in word or deed, do everything in the name of the Lord Jesus, giving thanks to God the Father through him."[11] So everything a believer says and does is to represent the will and witness of Jesus, the purpose and power of that Name, the humble glory displayed in Jesus's relationship with His Father. The scripture does not say we should do our own thing and attach the Name of Jesus to our plans. Rather we are to do everything in the Name of Jesus. Every action performed and oracle emitted is to bring honor to and serve the will of Jesus who Himself did and said everything similarly unto His Father.

Chapter 20

PULL QUOTES AS SUMMARY

In an attempt to summarize the salient points of this book, I have listed the pull quotes from each chapter. I present these to you, as I hope to do everything, in the Name of Jesus Christ.

Introduction

For all of us there is both a "now" and a "not yet" experience of God's Word.

Will we believe our experience or God's Word?

The promise requires a process.

The Word of God repeatedly focuses on the Name.

Chapter 1

Names establish and communicate identity.

The first name spoken occurred before creation.

Chapter 2

This is how we are created in God's image: we have ability to speak.

A name is given to establish a reference to an identity.

Chapter 3

Their names made them preachers with a message.

The Name Jesus was prescriptive and prophetic.

Your family name ultimately comes from God.

A person's name is to be guarded for who the person really is.

Chapter 4

Is this not power, the ability to directly purvey your feelings to someone by use of a name?

The gospel is to be preached to the whole creation, to every name, to every noun describing a person, place, or thing.

How much more power goes forth when Jesus calls out a name!

Peter's identity was revealed to him AFTER he professed who Jesus was.

Chapter 5

This Name encompasses His omnipresence, omniscience, and omnipotence.

It is not that Christ came into existence before Abraham did, but that He never came into being at all.

Using Jesus's Name in prayer and ministry ascribes to all of these truths.

Chapter 6

Everything and every time is NOW for God.

Light has an inherent "eternal now" quality.

Believers who live at any time in the span of history are connected to the great event that happened once in time.

Jesus's death and resurrection had retroactive and proleptic effects.

Chapter 7

The words that proceed out of the mouth come from the heart.

Using foul language brings foul upon oneself.

The Name of Jesus is powerful for those who know Him and submit to Him, but brings judgment upon those who do not.

Chapter 8

He is in charge, but He is not in control.

Some seem to embrace Jesus's way of the cross so closely so as to almost disregard or dismiss the victory of the resurrection.

Either we will bring our theology down to fit our experience or we will bring our experience subject to the Word of God.

Chapter 9

Jesus's blood brings us to heaven and Jesus's body brings heaven to us.

His blood purchased forgiveness of sins and eternal life; His body brought healing in this life.

It is possible to ask from God and simultaneously neglect or refuse His answer or provision because it comes through ordinary people around us.

Chapter 10

When believers effectively use the Name of Jesus, the same power that raised Jesus from the dead is employed.

The exalted Name of Jesus occurred at His death and resurrection.

This exalted Name is The Name given to the church.

Chapter 11

The eternal destiny for each human is vested in a Name.

This is not just believing in certain tenets; it is experiential.

Chapter 12

God has all power to do whatever He wishes, but He usually accomplishes His purposes through His people who obey Him.

The weapons of our warfare are divinely powerful for breaking down strongholds.

Church doctrine is not so holy if it is lacking the power of the Name of Jesus and the Kingdom of God.

Chapter 13

The authority and commission to use the Name of Jesus is sevenfold.

If you are a child of God, then you are an heir of God, a joint heir with Christ.

Chapter 14

When one wields the words of thanksgiving and forgiveness, the tides of eternity and the heart of God Almighty are moved.

There are no circumstances where it is not the will of God to give thanks.

A habit of thanksgiving causes the mind to be set on the things of the Spirit, bringing life and peace.

When we give thanks to God in the Name of Jesus Christ FOR everything, this moves the heart of God.

This is why we are told to give thanks *for all things*: because God works *all things* together for good.

Chapter 15

This great promise does not make God our puppet for us to manage and manipulate.

We can always come to Him to receive forgiveness, but for some the relationship never goes beyond this.

Keeping His commandments brings confidence in prayer.

"If one turns away his ear from hearing the law, even his prayer is an abomination" (Prov. 28.9).

He puts His desires in our heart so our desires are His desires.

There is no expression of confidence before God if there is no request of Him.

Chapter 16

It is the going and bearing fruit that empowers asking in the Name of Jesus.

When Christians go anywhere in this way and bear fruit, then the Father will give whatever is asked in the Name of Jesus.

It is not the circumstances of life that hold a person from following Jesus and going forth in His Name, rather it is a matter of the heart and will.

Chapter 17

There are at least five scriptures that clarify this Great Commission.

Chapter 18

To ignore this conflict between the Kingdom of Light and the kingdom of darkness does not attend to the commission given to believers in the Name of Jesus.

We need a biblical view of our country, not a cultural view of the Bible.

Believers will expel demons in the Name of Jesus.

The scriptures state that he who speaks in a tongue edifies himself.

Theologies can be argued but a testimony or demonstration of the power of God cuts through arguments.

Chapter 19

The natural and supernatural are both natural to God.

Our being is not based on our doings. Our doings come from our being.

What we do comes best from who we are.

Fruitful doing comes from an obedient relationship with God.

Those who DO in Jesus's Name will find that His words are true.

ABOUT THE AUTHOR

G reg Berglund is both an Ordained Pastor and a Medical Doctor. He works a full time position in an Emergency Department and continues his pastoral ministry in his home church. His training and experience in both fields brings a unique perspective as each discipline informs the other. He is known to state that the scientific and medical communities need faith and the faith communities need evidence which a scientific process can provide. As might be expected, Greg has a special interest in health and healing through both natural and supernatural means.

Greg has travelled throughout all 50 of the United States of America and to over 40 other countries. He has taught and ministered at conferences and seminars nationally and internationally. At such gatherings he is keen on giving time for the Holy Spirit to do or say what He wills. Seeing the ministry of Jesus which was both compassionate and demonstrative, Greg is unafraid to publically employ the word of God to minister healing, salvation, and the filling of the Holy Spirit's power.

Dr. Berglund has attended a total of 29 years of school. His grades were average in grade school and high school. He did not graduate in the top third of his high school class. In his first year of college he came into a living, faith relationship with God through Jesus Christ. At this time he acquired a hunger for the word of God. He memorized the Epistle of James shortly after his conversion experience. At that time his grades in college dramatically

215

improved so that he graduated Magna Cum Laude and went on to study in both Seminary and Medical School. Currently he has memorized seven books of the Bible (Ephesians, Philippians, Colossians, James, 1 Peter, 2 Peter, and 1 John) along with other chapters and many verses.

Greg had the privilege of portraying the role of Jesus Christ in a Passion Play that spanned 20 years of performances to a total of approximately 750,000 people. He has often said that the hundreds of times he was set up on a cross to portray Jesus's death was his opportunity to experience the profound truth that he himself was also crucified with Christ (Gal. 2.20). His favorite reflection on his role in this production was "I'm just another doctor trying to play God."

Dr. Berglund is available to speak at events, seminars, and conferences. He can be contacted at 651-331-9005 or gberglund@ comcast.net for such arrangements.

ENDNOTES

Introduction

1. John 15.16.
2. James 4.5.
3. John 15.16.
4. Ps. 113.2.

Chapter 1: The Need for a Name

1. Gen. 1.3.
2. Gen. 1.5.
3. Gen. 1.6.
4. Gen. 1.8.
5. Gen. 1.10.
6. Gen. 2.19.

Chapter 3: A Name's Functions

1. Ex. 15.23.
2. Gen. 21.31.
3. Num. 11.3.
4. Jezreel was the name of a very fertile plain in the tribe of Issachar, which was many times the scene of terrible struggles (Judg. 4:13; Judg. 6:33; Judg. 7:1; 1Sam. 29:1). It was also the name of a town associated with the guilt of Ahab and Jezebel in bringing about the murder of Naboth (1 Kings 21), and with the final extinction of Ahab's house by Jehu (2 Kg. 9:21; 2 Kg. 10:11).
5. Luke 1.5-25, 59-64.
6. Luke 1. 31-33.
7. Matt. 1.21.
8. The Rock, The Road, and the Rabbi, Kathie Lee Gifford with Rabbi Jason Sobel, 2018, W Publishing Group, pages 15-17.)

9. Matt. 19.5-6.
10. Eph. 3.14-15.
11. Ex. 20.7.
12. Ex. 20.16.

Chapter 4: The Power of Names

1. Matt. 17.20.
2. Luke 17.6.
3. Mark 16.15.
4. Rom. 8.19-23.
5. Luke 8.27-33.
6. Luke 6.13-16.
7. John 10.3.
8. Jesus calls his sheep by name. John 10.3: "…the sheep hear his voice, and he calls his own sheep by name and leads them out."
9. Luke 21.17.
10. John 15.4.
11. Expositions of Holy Scripture, Alexander MacLaren – biblesupport.com.
12. Luke 19.2-10.
13. Rev. 2.17.
14. Eph. 1.13-14.
15. Acts 2.21.
16. Rom. 10.13.
17. Matt. 9.27 and 20.30.

Chapter 5: Names for God

1. Is. 45.6.
2. Gen. 1.5.
3. Gen. 1.2.
4. See also Rom. 8.9-10 which uses synonymously the Names of the Triune God.
5. John 4.26.
6. https://www.blueletterbible.org/study/misc/name_god.cfm.
7. Prov. 18.10.
8. Luke 22.42.

Chapter 6: Eternal Now – I Am Who I Am

1. Rev. 1.4, 1.8, 4.8.

2. 2 Pet. 3.8.
3. 1 John 1.5.
4. John 8.12.
5. 1 John 2.9.
6. 1 John 2.9-11.
7. Gal. 2.20.

Chapter 7: In Vain

1. 1 Cor. 2.11.
2. Luke 6.45.
3. Eph. 5.4.
4. Rom. 12.14.
5. Luke 6.27-28.
6. Matt. 17.20.
7. Rev. 13.5-6.
8. Ex. 20.7.
9. 1 John 5.18.
10. John 3.36.
11. Luke 21.8.
12. Matt. 24.5.
13. 2 Pet. 2.18-19.

Chapter 8: Reducing The Name

1. 2 Pet. 3.13.
2. John 16.33.
3. Luke 10.38-42.
4. Eph. 4.21.
5. Col. 2.3.
6. John 15.5.

Chapter 9: Discern The Body

1. 1 Pet. 2.24.
2. Gal. 2.20, Col. 3.1-3.
3. There is no problem with the original scriptures in Isaiah and Matthew. These are accurate representations one of another and represent the heart and will of God as they are inspired by the Holy Spirit.
4. Eph. 5.23.
5. Luke 4.18-19.
6. Col. 3.3.

Chapter 10: Above Every Other Name

1. John 1.1-3.
2. Eph. 1.22.
3. John 1.1-3.
4. Eph. 4.9-10.
5. Eph. 1.22.

Chapter 11: In Jesus's Name

1. 1 Kg. 8.17, see also 1 Chron. 22.7.
2. Acts 2.21.
3. Acts 4.12.
4. Rev. 2.3.
5. Acts 5.28.
6. 1 Cor. 2.1-5.
7. John 15.4.

Chapter 12: Strategies for Use

1. Ex. 4.17.
2. 2 Cor. 10.3-5.
3. Acts 18.1.
4. 1 Cor. 4.20.

Chapter 13: Sevenfold Right To Use The Name

1. "You must be born anew" (John 3.7).
2. Matt. 28.18-20.

Chapter 14: Give Thanks

1. Jon. 2.10-11.
2. John 13.3.
3. Rom. 8.5-6.
4. Rev. 21.5.

Chapter 15: Ask in My Name

1. See James 4.1-3.
2. Rom. 8.1.
3. 2 Cor. 7.10.
4. John 15.3.

5. Rom. 8.1.
6. Heb. 4.16.
7. 1 Pet. 3.12.
8. Prov. 28.9.
9. 1 John 3.23.
10. Rom. 8.8.
11. Rom. 15.3.
12. Luke 3.22.
13. 1 John 3.18.
14. James 4.2.
15. Phil. 4.6.
16. Prov. 14.12.
17. Acts 22.14.
18. Eph. 3.3.
19. Col. 4.12.
20. John 7.17.
21. 1 John 5.14-15.

Chapter 16: Go in My Name

1. John 16.33.
2. Matt. 16.24.
3. Luke 14.27.
4. Matt. 9.35, see also Matt 4.23.

Chapter 18: Signs in Jesus's Name

1. 1 Cor. 14.20.
2. Eph. 6.12.
3. For more information on this subject see "Needless casualties of war" by John Paul Jackson.
4. 1 Cor. 14.4.
5. Joel 2.28-29.
6. Acts 2.38-39.
7. Rom. 8.26-27.
8. Mark 16.17.
9. 1 Cor. 14.21.
10. Gen. 11.4-9.
11. Acts 9.15-16.
12. John 16.33.
13. The Baptism of Jesse Taylor, recorded by the Oak Ridge Boys.

14. Rom. 8.11, Eph. 1.19.
15. 1 John 4.4.

Chapter 19: Do Everything

1. John 10.25.
2. Acts 3.6.
3. Acts 16.18.
4. Acts 4.30.
5. Matt. 17.20.
6. John 15.5.
7. 2 Cor. 5.17.
8. Col. 3.17.
9. John 7.17.
10. Rom. 8.28.
11. Col. 3.17.

CPSIA information can be obtained
at www.ICGtesting.com
Printed in the USA
FSHW021137080719
59791FS